"BANDOLEROS"

OUTLAWED GUERRILLAS
OF THE
PHILIPPINE-AMERICAN WAR
1903-1907

"BANDOLEROS"

OUTLAWED GUERRILLAS
OF THE
PHILIPPINE-AMERICAN WAR
1903-1907

ORLINO A. OCHOSA

New Day
Publishers

Quezon City, Philippines
1995

Cover Design: **Alfredo M. Punzalan**

Ochosa, Orlino A.
    Bandoleros: outlawed guerrillas
of the Philippine-American war 1903-1907/
Orlino A. Ochosa. - Quezon City: New Day Publishers,
c 1995
    184 pp.: ill
    Includes bibliography and index.

    1. San Miguel, Luciano. 2. Montalan, Julian.
3. Sakay, Macario Leon.
4. Guerrillas—Philippines—Biography.
. I. Title.

DS688.6A2 1995 959.9032'092 P954000112

ISBN 971-10-0555-7 (BP)

First Impression, 1995
Third Impression, 1999

Handog

kay

Soultwin

Such men as Sakay, Carreon, Montalan,
Ola, De Vega, Villafuerte, Natividad,
Despida, Estacio, Porto and Felizardo
carried on the guerrilla warfare for
many years, but naturally, their cause
having been finally defeated, their
names are not now held in grateful
remembrance . . .

—Claro M. Recto, 1946

Ang di nagsisukong ating gerilyero'y
hinuli't nginanlang mga "bandolero."

—Lope K. Santos, 1953

The guerrilla is like a poet.
He moves with the green brown
multitude . . .

—Jose Ma. Sison, 1968

ACKNOWLEDGMENTS

PROFESSOR ED B. GULL, American, Sagada elder, and author of the mythical *English Grammar in 405 Easy Lessons,* reciprocated my taking literary potshots at his countrymen by shooting back at my grammar with imperialist editorial gore. Sige, bodhisattva!

Advertising artist Fred Musni Punzalan, Batang Murphy, executive art director for Zorrilla & Partners, imposed a week-long moratorium on his *kriyetib* work to create the cover design for "Bandoleros." And another artist friend, Victor Pardo, Vigan Boy, selected the typography for the cover and interior titles, and took care of all final art.

Saturday Group painter Boi Sibug, Laking Tondo, professional adman, amateur photographer, and natural easyrider, a few years back sketched—*gratis con amor*—the pastel portrait that finally finds its well-deserved place on this book's back cover. And visualizer Norman Tioco, Tubong Navotas, a.k.a. "Papakol Kid," visualized three of our "bandits"—Sakay, Montalan and de Vega—for the pictorial essay, and not merely for art's sake.

Poet Herminio S. Beltran, Jr., Ilocano, past associate editor of *Diliman Review,* encouraged me in 1989 to contribute the Montalan portion of this book to their U.P. journal (whose permission to reprint is hereby gratefully acknowledged).

Bibliophile Maria Luisa Moral, Aklanon, as chief of the National Library Filipiniana and Asia Division, allowed us to use materials in their picture collections to illustrate all of this book's Pictorial Essay—with the sole exception of Luciano San Miguel's photograph on page 114, courtesy of the Ayala Museum Iconographic Archives. And camera-shooting "VG" Llagas, Bondoc peninsular, did wonderful photocopying work.

New Day editor Vesta B. Tolentino never tired of her meticulous pencil work, looking for lapses of all sorts and suggesting ways of improving the book in its content and form. Desktop man Alejandro Bulseco set the types and fixed the format, Denia Pascua read the proofs and helped prepare the index, while Loida de Vera laid out the pictures. All humbly said they merely did their job, but I must insist they did it with candor and patience—and smiles.

Retired New Day director Mrs. Gloria F. Rodriguez, Bacolod-non, inspired the completion of this book just by sincerely wishing it the best of luck. And her worthy successor, Bezalie P. Bautista, Tagalog, made that well-wish come true.

To them all: *Salamat!*

CONTENTS

PROLOGUE

REVOLUTION IS no dinner party and guerrilla war is no picnic. Thus did a once famous practitioner of the art serve a grim reminder for would-be advocates of revolution and guerrilla war, or a combination of both. And rightly so. In the pre-Maoist, even pre-Leninist era, we waged a war of national liberation against Spanish colonialism and then fought a classic guerrilla war against American imperialism—the first of its kind in all of Asia. Neither dinner party nor picnic, those terrible little wars made one long hell of a bloodletting orgy where one got "rubbed out" (to use the *yanqui* idiom) depending on a person's luck, or "sold out" depending on the man's persuasion. But because the whole thing was meant to give life to a just-born ideal called *nacionalismo*, the best men—cultured and unlettered—happily bled, even gave their lives for this first *Filipino* national enterprise.

The best men were not necessarily the most prominent names— not a Paterno, not a Buencamino or a Pardo de Tavera, maybe not even an Aguinaldo. The best of them fought and died—both in glory and in anonymity: the "katipuneros" of 1892-1896, the "insurrectos" of 1897-1902, and the "bandoleros" of 1903-1907.

Ideological considerations aside, the Philippine Revolution as a national independence movement was both expressly political and unconsciously social. Just as it was an indigenous people rising as a nation to liberate themselves from two colonizing powers, it was also the native "haves" and "have-nots," to use labels popularized by the late Teodoro Agoncillo, clashing for class leadership for the first time. Beneath the surface of what looked like national unity, social strata were incompatible with one another. The masses clashed with the middle class, and the middle class with the elite, thus contradicting the very principles of the Revolution and, no doubt, precipitating its fall.

Politically, the revolutionary period (1892-1907) is divided into two phases: first, the armed uprising and final victory against Spain, and second, the armed resistance fought and lost against America. But the social aspect divides the historical period into three phases.

The initial phase (1892-1896), though national in aspiration, was local in scope: strictly proletarian, specifically an affair of the working class of Tondo and its environs—even if we grant that its founding leaders were lower middle class, even if we grant that its later recruits in the provinces were largely *principalia* and *ilustrado*. From their ranks rose the plebeian ideologues, Andres Bonifacio and Emilio Jacinto, from whose revolutionary teachings the Katipunan envisioned not only national liberation from foreign rule but also, in the process, social transformation within. But the entry into the movement of the provincial gentry, led by the *principales* of Cavite, resulted in the preemption of the "revolt of the masses," as Agoncillo called it, and the leadership of the revolution passed from plebeian (as symbolized by Bonifacio) to petty middle class (in the person of *Don* Emilio Aguinaldo).

Though warlords lorded it over true warriors, the next phase (1897-1902) was *the* Revolution because, in spite of the clannish character of its leadership, it was a national movement of classes and tribes. Supported for a while by the *ilustrado* elite with whom they later got entangled, Aguinaldo's *revolucionarios* were the main cast in the attempt of their *republica* to put on a better and more sophisticated show (though sometimes overacted) than the dominantly plebeian Katipunan's. Emilio Jacinto, though he carried the fight in Laguna, was ignored (and 90 years after his death, we're still quite unsure what/who really killed him—and exactly where/why). So were the unlettered KKK generals who had started, and initially lost, the first libertarian battles: Mones Bautista, Francisco de los Santos, Apolonio Samson, Julian Santos, Faustino Guillermo—and yes, Francisco Carreon and Macario Sakay. Not even the revolutionary heroine of 1896, Tandang Sora, was spared by class snobbery: at no time in happier days of the Republic was there any initiative to liberate her from exile in Guam where she continued to languish long after Spain had been defeated (in fact, she was still there when the Americans, in turn, deported Mabini, Ricarte and other "irreconcilable" *republicanos* in 1901).

By 1902, the days of the Republic were over. Subdued by American arms, most of its leaders gave up the fight and began to compromise. The rich-creole-*ilustrado* elements even sold out to the new masters in utter subservience. But the end of the Republic was not the end of the Revolution, because the year the Americans officially declared its end—1902—merely marked the transition to the third and last phase (1903-1907) of the nationalist struggle of those times.

In Manila, the *katipuneros* and *insurrectos* of the recent wars reemerged as organized workers unions, church militants, and underground theater guilds leading the urban nationalist struggle against the *federalistas,* renegades of the second phase and snobs of the first and third phases. And in the countrysides, they reappeared as "bandoleros," so-called bands of brigands who had taken over the anti-American resistance abandoned by the generals of the Republic—"under the cloak of patriotism," as the colonial regime sneered at their intransigence.

This whole revolutionary period, a broad span of 15 years, started with the Katipunan—and ended with it. But the real significance here is this unbared historical truth: those last *bandolero* holdouts against American imperialism were also the first *katipunero* vanguards against Spanish colonialism!

Those who see history as a class conflict now argue that the Revolution which took place between 1897 and 1902 was national and democratic in form but not in outlook since the leadership was predominantly middle-class Tagalog and, therefore, neither national nor democratic. To them, 1892-1896 and again 1903-1907 were the real mass movements—proletarian-peasant movements suppressed by both *estrangero* and *hacendero* precisely because they were people-oriented and not in the interest of a vacillating, compromising elite. Be that as it may, 1897-1902 is part of our revolutionary history and to omit the period is to distort *that* history. Besides, important lessons on guerrilla warfare, good or bad, can be learned from every phase of our Revolution—lessons on revolution that predated Zapata or Lenin.

All revolutions have produced heroes as well as tyrants. And when tyrants finally seize power—either by winning the revolution or, if a loser, by selling it to the invader—most often the real heroes of the movement are obscured, vilified or replaced by personalities who represent or who are not inimical to the interests of both master and *tuta.*

Our Revolution, for instance, because we lost it through

compromise by those who could have best provided its leadership, has been written mainly on the deeds of the men who reneged on the movement. So-called leaders were enshrined in the national pantheon as "heroes" just because they were among the leading figures at the *height* of the Revolution, although they were also among the first ones to abandon it when its tide went down. Those who did not obey their "leaders," who did not abandon the struggle, and who refused to bend their knees in subservience to the new masters were called outlaws and bandits—"bandoleros"—for never renouncing the independence ideal they had been exhorted to defend with their lives. And it took a nationalist revival 60 years after the first nationalist struggle for the likes of Luciano San Miguel, Julian Montalan, and Macario Sakay—lesser known men of the Revolution, but not necessarily men of less fiber—to regain respectability in our own history books.

This is not to imply that the Revolution failed because the middle class leadership was merely a bunch of weaklings and opportunists. For there must surely have been as many plebeian fighters whose motivations were dubious as there were sincere bourgeois revolutionaries with firm nationalist convictions. From the *ilustrados* themselves originated such respected names as Alejandrino, Apacible, Almeida, Lukban, Magbanua, De los Reyes, Mabini—and, yes, Luna, who was liquidated for opposing a policy that sought peace with the Americans, and Malvar, who fought the longest republican resistance in Batangas, and Ricarte, who spent half of his lifetime in exile for refusing to swear and bow to American rule. They were all good and honest *ilustrados* who meant well; it is regrettable that they can be counted only on the fingers. For the predominating middle-class leadership was what that historian of the Philippine Left, Amado Guerrero, describes as "inadequate, flabby and compromising."

Even a Malvar would compromise.

SO WHO THEN, as Jonathan Fast and Jim Richardson posed the question in a recent work, were "the real heroes of the Revolution"? They offer an answer themselves:

> We maintain that the common people, unsung, unremembered, and cruelly betrayed, emerged as the true defenders of national honor. It would be charitable to suggest that their role in the anti-colonial struggle has been largely neglected. A more cynical but perhaps more accurate view is that the role of the

common people—who struggled against American hegemony for many years after the officers and gentlemen of Malolos had made their peace—had been consciously written out of the history of the nation by people—Americans and Filipinos alike—who had reason to be anxious that the story not be told.

On the next pages are profiles of three genuine people's heroes whose lives and labors, because uncompromisingly revolutionary, have been "consciously written out of history." All three of them were turn-of-the-century *indio* pioneers of revolutionary guerrilla war who were all outlawed and suppressed for defying American imperialist "benevolence" and discrediting local *americanista* collaboration for as long as they were able to—and long after the "last Filipino general to surrender" had indeed surrendered and abandoned the anti-American resistance.Their manners of dying— Luciano San Miguel on the battlefield, Macario Sakay at the gallows, and Julian Montalan simply dying in the minds of his own *kababayans*—summarize an "unofficial" period of our history denigrated and obliterated as the "bandit phase" of a war American Occupation made generations of Filipinos forget.

"*Bandoleros*," the book, germinated from my 1988 article "Himagsikan ng mga Tulisan" published in the *Diliman Review.* The original idea, as in "Tulisan," was to have Luciano San Miguel, Macario Sakay and Artemio Ricarte in the "bandit" gallery. It was only as an afterthought that I decided Julian Montalan should not be just a side story in the section on Sakay but a story all its own—first, because Montalan aptly represents the essential revolutionary peasant element of the Revolution (just as Sakay personifies Manila's working class and San Miguel the provincial commoner); second, because he really is as much a symbol of his times as Sakay was; and third, because it's about time the untold Montalan story was told fully, as near as possible to the obliterated truth, away from the American-made bandit legend. And one more reason for Ricarte's exclusion would be because Nick Joaquin, for one, in "When Stopped the Revolution?" in his *A Question of Heroes* (Ayala Museum, 1977), has already written at length and with depth on the Vibora. Anyway, I have tried to incorporate all Ricartista material pertinent to the "bandit" era whenever called for in all the three biographical sections of this book.

I have focused my study on the 1903-1907 struggle because, of the three phases of the Revolution I mentioned earlier, it is the period that has not yet been sufficiently told, except perhaps in the scholarly works of the historians Renato Constantino and Reynaldo C. Ileto in the 1970s. I have selected those three protagonists of that struggle because theirs are lives that are as interesting as they are controversial, and theirs are deserving biographies that have been scantily or feebly written, or never been written at all. And I have chosen the biographical approach on the "bandoleros," rather than making a case on the subject of *bandolerismo*, because I feel that this period can best be read and understood through the individual (yet often interlapping and interacting) revolutionary careers of these three unremembered Filipinos in one single volume.

Let us go back then to those suppressed years of the Philippine-American War for a second, closer look at its outlawed guerrilla heroes: the Bandoleros.

ORLINO A. OCHOSA
17 February 1992

1

SAN LUCIANO
SAN MIGUEL

**READING BETWEEN THE LINES
FOR THE HIDDEN HEROISM
OF THE "SANTO INSURRECTO"**

one

SAN LUCIANO SAN MIGUEL

Ricarte's Personal Hero

THE PHILIPPINE REVOLUTION should have ended in 1902, but did not. Holdouts of the Republic still held out; fighters for the revolutionary cause still fought it out. General Miguel Malvar should have been the last revolutionary leader to come down, but no. Long after Malvar turned in his revolver and dagger, and called upon the fighters to do the same, the Resistance he abandoned would still pulsate and still move in the persons of other generals and lesser leaders whom the Americans had all outlawed. The forces of occupation, though they had officially declared the war in the Philippines ended, were still to complete the work of "pacification" in 1903.

That war had taught Americans their early lessons about Filipinos. And one of the first things they learned was this: An effective way to "civilize 'em with the Krag" was to *arm some of them* with the Krag. And so the Philippine Constabulary and the Philippine Scouts came to be what the *Guardia Civil* had been during the Spanish rule. Their common reason for being was chiefly as a reaction to freedomwish, once national and democratic, now confined to a few provinces infested by "ladrones." In 1902-1903, according to American author Vic Hurley, "the most serious menace to the peace of the Philippine Islands . . . was the insurgent General Luciano San Miguel."

Hurley wrote *Jungle Patrol*, a book on the early exploits of the Philippine Constabulary under the Americans. Here he devotes ten pages on General San Miguel's daring guerrilla activities and heroic death. Said Hurley of that revolutionary fighter:

3

He was an extremely able leader. . . . There was a certain honesty in his convictions and he was respected by the [U.S.] Army and Constabulary officers who pursued him. . . . *San Miguel must be rated a sincere insurgent and not a bandit.* [Underscoring supplied]

Hurley, of course, writes long after San Miguel was dead and he speaks of a period of the Revolution that had, for the American authorities and the native *ilustrados* who accepted their rule, already lost its "respectability"—the "ladrone" phase, as it is known in American archives. That was the period of suppressed Filipino nationalism, those early American "empire days" when Filipinos were getting their first colonial brainwash. There were no more *patrioticos* working for independence. There were now only crackpots and opportunists like Ricarte, murderers and assassins like Sakay, bandits and outlaws like San Miguel.

But Hurley, at least, rates San Miguel as "a sincere insurrecto."

Luciano San Miguel, not Miguel Malvar, was indeed the last bonafide "insurrecto" general under Aguinaldo's Republic to remain in the field against the Americans at a time when Artemio Ricarte "Vibora" was still an exile in Guam. Recall that Lukban surrendered in Samar in February 1902. This was followed by the surrender of Noriel in Cavite the following month and, finally, by those of Guevarra's in Leyte and of Malvar's in Batangas in April of that year.

But that is not the point. The more important fact is that San Miguel, like Ricarte, *never* accepted the American rule. But while Ricarte languished in forced exile, San Miguel fought to his last dying breath in a bloody battle near Marikina in 1903. Ricarte from that time on, in letters and manifestoes from Hongkong, always referred to him as "the hero General Luciano San Miguel."

And yet, where he died (Corral-na-Bato) and when he died (27 March) are nowhere read by Filipinos on the pages of their history, nor his death even remembered in song as that of a hero's.

It is rather curious how even as a controversial war hero, General San Miguel's identity can remain remote for so long. His biography has yet to be written. Galang's *Encyclopaedia of the Philippines* is probably the only book that honors him, for lack of any other biography, with this feeble "citation"—underscoring and exclamation marks supplied—under the heading of "Hero Martyrs":

4

SAN MIGUEL, LUCIANO

General. Bravely fought and was wounded in Batangas. Hero-like, he exposed himself to danger during the Revolution. Survived the battles and *died in peace*[!!!].

Yet, one digs for facts and gets the impression that Luciano San Miguel is one revolutionary figure whose name has to be repeated again and again in any worthwhile history of the Revolution.

And San Miguel was a leading figure in *all* of its phases.

Let's go back to the first phase of the revolution in Cavite. Like Malvar, Ricarte and other prominent generals of the Republic who fought against both Spaniards and Americans, San Miguel served the Revolution from its earliest campaigns in 1896-1897. He was one of the stalwarts in the *Magdiwang* Council, or the pro-Bonifacio wing, of the Katipunan in Cavite headed by General Santiago Alvarez (who didn't fight under the Republic).

San Miguel's early exploits in Cavite and Batangas are told in the separate memoirs of Generals Ricarte and Alvarez. In Batangas, he was "Koronel San Miguel"—second in command in the brigade of General Eleuterio Marasigan (who didn't remain a general under the Republic either). While his superior officer was out with the main force to lay siege on the town of Balayan, San Miguel defended Nasugbu with a few men when it was attacked by a strong Spanish force under Colonel Pazos. The enemy captured Nasugbu but not until the rebels were almost wiped out with not more than five survivors, one of them San Miguel.

For his bravery, the *Magdiwang* hierarchy rewarded San Miguel with a promotion to the rank of brigadier-general and a frontline command in Cavite. But his rank was later revoked and he was relegated back to colonel upon the reorganization of the rebel forces under Aguinaldo's overall command, prior to the armistice of Biyak-na-Bato. At any rate, it was as a general of the *Magdiwang* army that he attended the fateful Tejeros Convention in March 1897.

San Miguel had always been a good *Magdiwang* man. He may even have been a rabid *Bonifacista*. But it became clear later that his services were not dedicated to a single man or to a single faction alone when it concerned the entire revolution and country. For instance, a near civil war with Aguinaldo's *Magdalo* forces as a

5

result of the court-martial of Andres Bonifacio in April was closely averted, thanks to his (and Santiago Alvarez's) pacification efforts and appeal for unity in the revolutionary ranks. *Magdiwang* hotheads were for attacking the *Magdalo* headquarters, in Naic, to rescue the *Supremo* from prison. But San Miguel and Alvarez were two among broadminds: they would have no part in any bloody plan which would lead the Revolution to nowhere but its fall.

Alvarez himself, in his memoirs, explains why he—and Luciano San Miguel—acted the way they did:

> What good will a few comrades get for breaking up and fighting among themselves? If that happens, the thick ranks of the enemy will pass victoriously over our own follies, for we will be defenseless against them because of evil intrigues, of brother subjugating another brother, when our blood and our lives should be consecrated to no other purpose but the *Kalayaan ng Inang Bayan*.

San Miguel's adherence to *amor patria* over "cronyism" only revealed his convictions as a true revolutionary, a true patriot, and even a true Katipunero—though he, like the Alvarezes and Ricarte, would let the Father of the Katipunan die, for the Revolution to survive.

Earlier, in March, it was his conduct as a true rebel fighter that San Miguel displayed in the field of battle. He had supervised the defense of the rebel trenches in San Francisco de Malabon from the onslaughts of Spanish General Lachambre's troops. Assisted by Colonel Esteban San Juan, Lieutenant-Colonel Antonio Virata, and Major Julian Montalan (the Montalan who, like him, would carry on the anti-American resistance after 1902), San Miguel's command foiled the enemy's initial thrusts and drove them back to Noveleta. It was not until the first week of April that San Francisco de Malabon was finally captured by the Spanish forces, but only after a bloody close-quarter fighting right in the trenches.

There is no record to show that San Miguel favored the Pact of Biyak-na-Bato, or that he ceased operations after Aguinaldo and his companions left for Hongkong, or that he received any money paid by the Spanish government in accordance with the provisions of the pact. What is certain is this: When Aguinaldo returned to the Philippines on 19 May 1898 to renew the Revolution, San Miguel was the first senior officer to report for duty, immediately on the next day.

Aguinaldo recounted in his *True Version of the Revolution:* "On the night of that day—the 20th of May—the old revolutionary chief, Señor Luciano San Miguel, today [23 September 1899] brigadier-general, presented himself to me to receive orders, which were given to him . . ."

The historian Teodoro Agoncillo writes in *Malolos: The Crisis of the Republic:* "Aguinaldo immediately ordered him to take charge of the projected revolt in the provinces of Manila, Laguna, Batangas, Morong (Rizal), Bulacan, Pampanga, Tarlak, Nueva Ecija and other provinces in the north, and he went forth that night to execute them."

Military commentator Uldarico Baclagon attributes the clean-up drive against the Spanish forces in Cavite to San Miguel's troops. An excerpt from his *Philippine Campaigns* follows:

Cavite being the seat of the revolutionary government, the first step taken by the rebels was to clean up that province of all Spaniards. This was undertaken by troops under the command of Col. Luciano San Miguel who captured and occupied the towns of Caridad, San Roque and Cavite Viejo (Kawit). Col. San Miguel's force, attacking in seven columns, captured about 1,000 prisoners and numerous arms, including cannons.

And Teodoro Kalaw, in his *Philippine Revolution*, adds these commendatory words: "Thanks to the services of these columns [commanded by San Miguel], there were no cases of outrages of any kind or public disorder committed either by American soldiers or any other persons."

In this second phase of the Revolution, as in the first, San Miguel was among its principal characters, one of its outstanding warriors. The Katipunan, in the persons of the *Bonifacistas*, had dropped out of the first revolution. But San Miguel was the first man of that group to discard factionalism by inaugurating the next war of 1898. Today, personalities of lesser stature have schools and streets, or even towns, named after them. But, again like Ricarte, and except perhaps for a street in Caloocan, there is nothing for Luciano San Miguel.

Under the Republic

MEN OF *MAGDALO* would take over to finish the revolution a *Magdiwang* man had inaugurated—that was the irony of it for Luciano San Miguel in 1898. His fine work was not given its just reward after *independencia* was declared in June. He was not made a general to command any of the expeditionary forces sent to liberate the provinces. He was not even named to command any of the four Filipino zones in the siege of Manila.

In the siege of Manila, San Miguel was only second-in-command to General Pio del Pilar in the Second Zone, with headquarters in San Pedro Makati. It was only after the fall of Manila and after General Montenegro was ousted for misconduct, that Aguinaldo assigned the Third Zone to him (though he remained a Colonel). San Miguel was assisted in his work in the Third Zone by Lieutenant-Colonel Hermogenes Bautista and Major Fernando E. Grey. His command consisted of a mixed force of eight companies, detached from the following provincial battalions:

Pangasinan	3 companies
Pampanga	2 companies
Tarlac	1 company
Morong	1 company
Manila (Fourth Zone)	1 company

These troops were scattered in San Juan del Monte, San Francisco del Monte, San Felipe Neri, Santolan, Marikina, San Mateo, and Montalban. They were a curious mixture of Katipunan veterans, second-generation *revolucionarios*, deserters of the Spanish Volunteer Militia, "Gabinista" followers from Pampanga, *remontado* tribesmen from the Morong mountains, and maybe even a few "Guardia de Honor" fanatics from Pangasinan. It was a coming together more democratic, perhaps, than the very crowd that proclaimed Philippine independence at Kawit.

The most critical area in the Third Zone was San Juan del Monte, particularly near the San Juan Bridge in Santa Mesa near where Blockhouses No. 6 and No. 7 were located. Colonel San Miguel, however, chose to set up his headquarters in the neighboring district of Mandaluyong, where he also put up a first-aid station for use of all the zones, in anticipation of armed conflict with the Americans. San Miguel's troops were holding these positions when the expected hostilities broke out on 4 February 1899. In fact, they fought the very first battle of the Philippine-American War.

The insult-throwing incidents that led to that shooting war are depicted 60 years after by American author Leon Wolff in *Little Brown Brother.*

At 8:30 p.m., February 4, 1899, Private William W. Grayson of Company B, First Nebraska Volunteers, was patrolling his regimental outpost near Santa Mesa. . . . The patrol of which Grayson was a unit had orders, in fact, to shoot any Filipino soldier who might try to enter the neutral area which separated the two armies. Only two days ago Brigadier-General Arthur MacArthur [who would be Military Governor] had warned Colonel San Miguel in unmistakable terms concerning such boundary violations, and the Philippine officer had promised to restrain his troops. This sort of thing had been going on for some months, however, with both sides violating the zone freely. The Nebraskans had been exchanging particularly acrid insults with the Filipino insurgents, for the American camp protruded sharply into the bend of the San Juan River and was surrounded on three sides by the native army.

. . . The Nebraskans had recently moved from barracks in the damp Binondo district to high, sandy ground near Santa Mesa. . . . . It was commanded by a young, tough West Pointer named Colonel Stotsenburg, who had been warned by General MacArthur that his position was extremely exposed and more vulnerable to attack than any other along the American perimeter. Nevertheless the former had lately advanced his outpost a trifle and had been having especially vehement arguments with Colonel San Miguel during the past few days. Late in January, he had called for additional artillery, and two guns of the Utah Battery had been emplaced three hundred yards behind the San Juan Bridge.

We are familiar with the American version of how the war began. We know it from their sources that it was that sentinel of the First Nebraskans, Private Willie Grayson, who started it all at the San Juan Bridge when he fired his Springfield on the "insurgent" patrol that tried to cross over. We learn now from the "insurrecto papers" who those unlucky Filipinos were whom Grayson had fired at: *Cabo* Anastacio Felix and two *soldados* of the 4th Company, Morong Battalion. This company was commanded by Captain Serapio Narvaez, who had his command post at the Polvorin (powder house) of San Juan.

When Private Grayson fired the first shot of the war that night of February 4th at San Juan Bridge, Colonel San Miguel was in Malolos "paying homage to Terpsichore," in the words of Dr. Santiago Barcelona. It was not until the following day, 5 February, that he arrived in his post to personally lead his troops in driving back the Americans. Nevertheless, without his supervision, his troops at Santa Mesa had fought very well during the night, making repeated attempts to cross the old stone bridge into Stotsenburg's zone—keeping the Americans there extremely worried until the morning came. As of 4 a.m. San Miguel's third chief, Major Grey, who was left in command in Mandaluyong, wired his zone commander in Malolos that "every man [is] holding his post with enthusiasm."

At the compromised Santa Mesa area, Captains Serapio Narvaez and Vicente Ramos led their companies across the San Juan River, pushed Grayson's outfit some distance back, even capturing an artillery piece abandoned by the surprised Americans. But after daybreak of the 5th, Colonel Stotsenburg's Nebraska regiment with two Colorado companies counterattacked and captured Blockhouses No. 6 and No. 7 from their Filipino defenders. Major Grey brought in his troops from Mandaluyong to assist in the defense of San Juan. But the Filipinos soon ran out of ammunition and all the troops were forced to engage in a series of running fights from the Polvorin, to the Deposito, to Cubao, and then to Marikina.

Captain John R.M. Taylor, compiler of the "insurrecto papers," quotes this eyewitness report: "From the Ermitaño Bridge [in San Juan] first, and later from the neighboring barrio of Cubao, I saw the retreat of our troops on Sunday morning [of the 5th]; at noon, I saw them fleeing utterly disorganized."

Colonel San Miguel arrived in Marikina that afternoon to find many of his men mixed with other units. He would find out that his Morong troops had gone as far as Cainta, Taytay, and Antipolo to rejoin their mother battalion under Colonel Lazaro Macapagal Lacandola, and Major Grey had joined the Pio del Pilar Brigade. But he also learned that his reserves under Colonel Mones Bautista were intact in San Mateo, and his Tarlac and Pangasinan troops had not abandoned their trenches in San Francisco del Monte.

Patiently, San Miguel gathered back his fighters. And during the first week of March he renewed actions in an attempt to regain lost ground and recapture, at least, the Deposito area in San Juan. These attempts kept on until 7 March, when Brigadier-General Irving Hale, commanding the American forces facing the Filipino Third Zone, ordered a three-sided attack that was

10

successful in driving back San Miguel's troops towards San Francisco del Monte. Here, on 25 March, the Nebraskans drove the Filipinos from their trenches only after a bitter hand-to-hand fight reminiscent of San Miguel's great defense of San Francisco de Malabon against the Spaniards in 1897.

The American correspondent Karl Irving Faust saw this bloody action and in his compilation of *Campaigning in the Philippines,* he reported the death of "an old man from Tarlac, who cried for water and a priest." Faust wrote:

His leg was shattered by a Springfield bullet, and he said he felt the chill of death. Through an interpreter we listened to his confession. He told us he had a wife and five children at Tarlac, and his last words were, "Forgive me for fighting the Americans, I did not know the kind of people they were."

The remnants of San Miguel's troops contested every inch of ground along the Novaliches Road—at Cabatuan, at Talipapa, then at the Tuliahan River—against the 4th U.S. Cavalry, the Utah Battery, the Pennsylvanians, and the Nebraskans that made up General Hale's brigade. Colonel Bautista's reserves in San Mateo, mostly bolomen, tried to support their beaten and fleeing comrades with sorties made during the night against General Hale's rear, but without success, as one might expect.

After these actions, San Miguel was relieved of his command over the Third Zone by General Licerio Geronimo.

As one of the units incorporated into the Luna Division, the remnants of San Miguel's forces were in the thick of the Bulacan campaigns. Perhaps it is one of the ironies of war that San Miguel and his men would participate in the Battle of Quingua in April. There they clashed again with their old enemies—Colonel John Stotsenburg and his Nebraska Volunteers. And sweet revenge was theirs, for in this fight which lasted for two days—one of the bloodiest battles of the Philippine-American War—the Nebraskans lost their "young, tough West Pointer."

In May, Aguinaldo placed Colonel San Miguel in command of the newly activated "Zambales Battalion." This was the force of "katipunized" *provincianos* in northern Zambales who did not lay down their arms after the peace of Biyak-na-Bato and who, all by themselves, liberated that region in 1898, including parts of Pangasinan and La Union. But on the arrival of the Americans (and

11

Aguinaldo) their "general" Roman Manalang made the mistake of sending a letter to "The American General," offering his services and asking to be sold 2,000 rifles, which Taylor later found among Aguinaldo's "insurrecto papers." This explains why Aguinaldo's government became paranoid enough to have the Zambales rebels disarmed, and their leaders jailed, by the "expeditionary forces" in 1898. But times and tempers had changed in 1899, when Luna was even using Creole officers and troops to fight the Americans. The Malolos government gave Roman Manalang the regular rank of Lieutenant-Colonel in the Army of the Republic, and he was allowed to regroup and rearm his old officers and men.

Lieutenant-Colonel Manalang was second-in-command, Lieutenant-Colonel Juan Elveña was chief of staff, and Major Mauro Ortiz (another "general" deposed in 1898) was field commander of San Miguel's Zambales Battalion formed out of four regular rifle companies and five *sandatahan* (bolo) companies under the following officers:

Captain Urbano Virata	1st Company
Captain Moises Abueg	2nd Company
Captain Eulogio Miranda	3rd Company
Captain Vicente Espada	4th Company(*)
Captain Martin Basa	5th, 6th, 7th, 8th and 9th Companies of *Sandatahanes*

Initially, this battalion was assigned in Nueva Ecija and made good showing in a few skirmishes obviously meant to season the men. But later events would tend to show that the activation of the Zambales Battalion, and San Miguel's taking command of it, had something to do with the murder plot against Antonio Luna.

San Miguel may or may not have had any direct participation in the killing of General Luna. But if he did, it might do well to remember the same convictions San Miguel expressed in a similar

---

(*)To this company belonged Lieutenant Francisco Frani of Bulacan who later became a guerrilla hero hanged by the Americans, and Lieutenant Felipe Quintos of Alaminos who wrote in 1947 his memoirs of the revolution in Zambales, on which this data was based.

12

situation involving Bonifacio in 1897. At any rate, after Luna's death, Aguinaldo personally elevated Luciano San Miguel to Brigadier-General of the Filipino Army.

His Zambales troops were among those that marched in review before Aguinaldo's new headquarters in Angeles on 12 June, a week after Luna's death in Cabanatuan, on the occasion of the first anniversary of the Declaration of Philippine Independence at Kawit. For Luciano San Miguel, the ex-*Magdiwang*, it was also his first year of service under the Republic.

The San Miguel Brigade

THE SAN MIGUEL BRIGADE was a provisional one. From Taylor's documentary exhibits, we learn of its composition and exploits. Its nucleus was, of course, the troops of the Zambales Battalion now commanded by Colonel Roman Manalang. The Gapan (Nueva Ecija) Volunteers under Colonel Urbano Lacuna and the celebrated Kawit Battalion under Colonel Agapito Bonzon served as its auxilliary units.

These troops occupied the central defense line of San Fernando de Pampanga, with General San Miguel's brigade headquarters located in the barrio of Calulut. On its right flank at Bacolor was the Mascardo Brigade, and on its left in Mexico was the Aquino Brigade. The entire defense line was personally directed by General Aguinaldo himself who, on 16 June, ordered a general attack by these forces on San Fernando, then occupied by the American division commanded by now Major-General Arthur MacArthur.

Throughout June and July, the San Miguel Brigade took part in small sorties and skirmishes that were meant only to annoy the Americans in their lines.

During the second week of August, the Americans attacked in force, driving General San Miguel out of his headquarters in Calulut. His brigade fell back to Angeles which the Americans next tried to take on 10 August, in a fierce fight that lasted for ten hours. San Miguel held on to his position until the next day, when he ordered a tactical retreat to station his troops again on the Porac-Magalang Road. In cooperation with the troops of General Serviliano Aquino, who did a successful flank attack on the enemy, the San Miguel Brigade was able to recover Angeles on 12 August. In the American counterattack on the next day, the 13th, which lasted from 8 a.m. to 2 p.m., General San Miguel and his soldiers stopped fighting only after the front lines had exhausted their munitions. But the Kawit Battalion soon joined the fray, forced the Americans to retreat, and pursued them up to their own lines—in an admirable exercise of *good* "cavitismo." The Americans finally occupied Angeles again on 17 August—and that was because the San Miguel Brigade had run out of bullets to fight them.

One Luna partisan, Brigadier-General Venancio Concepcion, an *ilustrado* from Iloilo who later became chief-of-staff of the Filipino Army in retreat (though he surrendered soon after his appointment), criticized San Miguel, among other generals of 1896, for his "cavitismo" during this period of the war. It probably all started when Concepcion was deposed, following Luna's death, and relieved of his command by the just-promoted San Miguel. Now, late in August 1899, Aguinaldo had ordered Concepcion back to the front and named him chief-of-operations in the so-called "Paruao Line" around Bamban in Tarlac. This line was immediately behind San Miguel's own new positions on the north banks of the Abacan River, where he had entrenched his troops after the retreat from Angeles.

"I had understood," complained Concepcion to Aguinaldo soon afterwards, "that Señor San Miguel on learning of my presence here, ordered [his officers] to abstain from receiving orders from me."

When Concepcion asked that Bonzon's Kawit Battalion be sent to join an attack, these troops did not come. In retaliation, when San Miguel suggested that a simultaneous attack be made to recover Angeles, Concepcion objected on the ground that he did not conform with San Miguel's tactics.

The Paruao River Line was Aguinaldo's own project, which he patterned after the famous "Evangelista trenches" with his own improvements learned from the 1896 experience in Cavite. He had ordered it constructed soon after Luna's own Bagbag River Line fell, hoping to make the Americans bleed through its bamboo palisades, and didn't want those plans to miscarry now. Not that Aguinaldo was determined to carry on the war against the Americans through big pitched battles. The truth is, in the months following the Luna affair, especially after his own massive but fruitless attack on San Fernando in June, Aguinaldo saw the futility of holding the Central Plains against the onslaughts of the American advance. That was why he had proceeded, in accordance with Luna's original plans, with a scheme to turn the surrounding mountains into veritable strongholds from which to carry on the war through guerrilla warfare. The Paruao River Line was only meant to delay the American advance longer, while the guerrillas dispersed and got organized.

But Luna's previous assassination had created ill sentiments among "Lunistas" in the North—where Aguinaldo's only salvation lay—so that the President of the Republic thought it best to have that region paved first by men of his confidence. The men of 1896 and of Cavite, Aguinaldo must have thought, would be loyal to him to the end. For this purpose he had already named an 1896 general, Pio del Pilar, chief of operations in Bulacan in "all the country situated to the right of the railroad on the side of Manila." And for the province of Zambales, Aguinaldo's man was none other than the veteran 1896 Cavite warrior, Luciano San Miguel.

Zambales was one of the areas affected by popular discontent against the *republica*. Yet, contrary to some views, this did not mean that the province had ever been against the Revolution. In 1897, for example, the Zambaleños never ceased fighting even after the truce of Biyak-na-Bato. And when General Francisco Makabulos formed the provisional "Central Committee" in April 1898, the Zambales rebels were one in sentiment with their "brothers" in the central plains. This 1898 phase of the Revolution in Central Luzon was the troubled side of the "peace" of Biyak-na-Bato during that interim between the "first war" of 1896-97 and the "second war" of 1898.

Biographers of Makabulos missed this high point of his revolutionary career. Perhaps no other local leader had ever succeeded as he did in bringing about unity among so many factions and groups—radical *republicanos* like himself (radical, as distinguished from those who readily accepted compromise), original Katipuneros like Valentin Diaz, "katipunized" *provincianos* like Gregorio Mayor of Pangasinan and Roman Manalang of Zambales, and even religious "fanatics" like Felipe Salvador (*Santa Iglesia*) and Vicente del Prado (*Guardia de Honor*). These plural elements of the Revolution coming together in one glorious mass action at Dagupan in July 1898 certainly dwarfed the scenario and fanfare of the *republica* returning from "exile" to declare Philippine independence at Kawit the previous month. To some degree it was

15

matched only by the spectacle of a former *Magdiwang* man, Luciano San Miguel, rallying the *Magdalo* forces for the 1898 revolution in Cavite.

As provided for in its constitution, the ·comite central was dissolved after the Republic was restored. Then, the Republic sent out those expeditionary forces to claim the provinces in its name. Then, the old fears and intrigues that had destroyed the "first war" surfaced again. Part of the Manalang forces that had liberated northern Zambales had gone farther north, led by Mauro Ortiz, to sow the seeds of its own brand of revolution in La Union. They got there before General Tinio's expeditionary forces from Nueva Ecija arrived; then, together with them, they effected the surrender of the Spanish garrison at San Fernando. And then the clashes between Novo-Ecijanos and Zambaleños began. In the end, Ortiz and his men were disarmed and imprisoned. And elsewhere the *Santa Iglesia*, the *Guardias de Honor*, and the Katipunan followers who had prepared the groundwork for the second revolution would get the same shabby treatment from the armies of the *republica*. Thus, it should surprise no one that in the next war—against the Americans—the provinces of Tarlac, Pangasinan, Zambales and, because of Luna's death, Ilocos would become hotbeds of dissidence against the Republic.

Thus, when Colonel Pepito Leyba got separated from Aguinaldo's retreating column, he would mysteriously disappear in northern Pangasinan. When General Jose Alejandrino was trying to elude his American pursuers after a fight in Mangatarem, he would be chased and attacked by unknown bands of bolomen in Zambales. When Colonel Juan Gutierrez formed his guerrillas in La Union, he would be shocked to learn that some Ilocanos in the southern towns of his zone had organized themselves not to fight the *americanos* but to exterminate his guerrillas. Were they aggrieved Manalang followers seeking vengeance? Was it the Santa Iglesia striking back? The Guardias de Honor running amok? Perhaps the saddest fact of all was that even the charismatic Makabulos of Tarlac would not now be spared from the wrath of those anti-Republic dissenters.

But Zambales was important to the revolutionary command: its mountain ranges had been projected as an evacuation zone and base area for guerrillas the moment Tarlac fell. And so, to the Zambales Mountains Luciano San Miguel made haste that last quarter of 1899 and there promptly laid the groundwork for guerrilla warfare.

His provisional brigade of Caviteños, Novo-Ecijanos and Zambaleños had now been reduced to only the latter troops, as Lacuna's Gapan Volunteers had been sent home to Nueva Ecija and Bonzon's Kawit troops had been recalled as Aguinaldo's personal bodyguard. Manalang's Zambales Battalion, which San Miguel himself had occasion to serve as commander, nevertheless served as the key to the safe conduct of San Miguel, who was a nonnative of that region of revolutionary malcontents and, worse, a Caviteño. And as for the success of his guerrilla war in Zambales, San Miguel initiated the revival of the Katipunan in its old content and form, a pattern other guerrilla zone commanders would later (but that would be much later) imitate.

From the "insurrecto papers," John R.M. Taylor quotes San Miguel's first manifesto in Zambales, dated 6 December 1899:

> From this date I authorize the local presidentes to form the old Katipunan by kneeling before a crucifix and swearing not to be traitors to their country and to defend our rights unto the last drop of blood, after which, said oath will be signed with their own blood. . . . Those who do not conform to this order shall be considered enemies and their conduct shall be watched until evidence of being such shall have been obtained and they shall be tried by a court-martial made up of the same brothers. Everyone shall provide arms of all kinds for attacking the enemy. The brothers who may remain within the enemy's territory [that is, towns] shall furnish information and provisions to those who remain outside, and the widows and orphans of the brothers shall be protected by the same brothers. . . . The exclusive duty of brothers shall be to exterminate the enemy, true unity and fraternity. . . . Those who rob and abuse women shall be shot; if they are officers they shall be tried by a court-martial.

Aguinaldo's own proclamation instituting guerrilla warfare was issued at Bayambang, not very far from San Miguel's camp in Alaminos, earlier on 12 November. In that circular, Aguinaldo said nothing about Katipunan revival or anything of that sort. Had General San Miguel acted on his own in this effort to revive the Katipunan in Zambales?

He certainly did, and this is clear in his letter to Aguinaldo, then already in the north, on 8 December. In his letter, perhaps anticipating a reprimand for his act, Luciano San Miguel tried to explain his reasons for falling back to the Katipunan ideal:

I am at present devoting my efforts to exciting the patriotism of the people [of Zambales] and propagating the Katipunan, in order that, by this means, I may be able to avoid robbery, rape and many other like acts [that might be] committed in the moment of confusion when by bad luck (which God forbid) we should lose this province. I am also at present sending out orders and communications to the civil as well as the military authorities in the towns of the province of Pangasinan, so that order may be maintained and to either wipe out or win over the disaffected, the guards of honor [Guardias de Honor] and "tulisanes" which abound in that locality.

At the same time, San Miguel informed the Hongkong Committee of his intentions. "If I still had my brigade something might perhaps be accomplished," he told its members. But with only a handful of riflemen to start guerrilla warfare from scratch in Zambales, he implied to the *paisanos* in Hongkong the need to revert to the Katipunan in order that he might be able to create a mass base successfully in that Tagalog-hostile area. Accordingly, San Miguel proceeded to communicate with the people of Pangasinan and Zambales, even as American troops were scouring the towns in search of him.

From Alaminos on that same day of 8 December, he wrote to the guerrilla chief of Salasa: "You should immediately organize the Katipunan of that town in order that you may be in a position to defend your town as soon as possible, and even though it be with knives, arrows and lances the members of the Katipunan society can defend themselves very well."

On 13 December, still from Alaminos, he wrote to Valentin Diaz in Lingayen:

My dear brother and compañero: I . . . do not doubt that you will aid me in spreading the Katipunan, if the same, as our duty, has not already been accomplished by you since the moment that the Americans arrived there. It is almost certain that this society will bring us victory. Had not the Katipunan been abolished, the war would have been terminated and there would be now no small independent or disaffected parties, the members of which, nearly all of them, worked hard exposing their lives to the first and second insurrections. The consequence was just what was to be expected, as you well know. The town people did not, as a matter of fact, respond at the time [before the guerrilla war] and if the war has been kept up until now, it is due solely to the energy of the [nationalist] generals.

San Miguel was, of course, one of "the generals." He knew that Valentin Diaz was one of the original Katipuneros in 1892 (another

18

was Ladislao Diwa in Cavite) who continued to fight under the Republic. Diaz had been serving the Cause for almost a decade and yet he never attained the rank of general; it is even more curious that he was a colonel in 1897-1898, when he fought with Makabulos, but was now only a *comandante* at the time San Miguel wrote him. And yet, titles aside, Valentin Diaz was recognized as one of the more influential local leaders in western Pangasinan (though he himself was an Ilocano from Paoay who grew up in *eastern* Pangasinan). While San Miguel did not negate his own capability to carry on the war as a general of the Republic, he was saying, however, that he would be helpless without the assistance and support of local leaders of the calibre of Diaz. His letter continues:

There are some of our brothers who, in place of protecting the people, have meddled in affairs which do not concern them and asserted their authority without remembering that the people are groaning in a worse state now than when they were under the Spanish yoke, and those brothers of ours have not remembered that if we have worked, it was in the interest of the people, and also without remembering that the deceit would sooner or later be found out—that deceit commonly called politics—and also without remembering that the most powerful, the highest in office and the most valiant may be punished by the will of the people, which is omnipotent and inevitable.

In short, we, together with them—or better said, the people—are the ones who must rectify these evils and place things in preparation for the first opportunity.

I have already given an account to the Honorable President [i.e., Aguinaldo] of the circulars which have been distributed in that province [meaning Pangasinan], and which you have perhaps read.

It is not my desire to govern that province because I am not even able to look after this one [meaning Zambales], but the circumstances and my duty obliged me to do it after an understanding with General Alejandrino, who is at present sick in the southern part of this province; therefore, I trust that the people of that province will not be unfavorably disposed towards my instructions.

And finally, on 16 December, he circularized the "presidentes from Bolinao to Subic"—and here, San Miguel seemed indeed like a Bonifacio rising again to appeal to his Katipuneros:

You will . . . endeavor, brothers, to instill in your hearts the true love of country, genuine self-respect and spotless affection for our native land which groans for its loyal inhabitants and do not permit it to fall into the clutches of the malignant invader. . . .

19

Soon after San Miguel issued his orders, the Katipunan idea spread quickly throughout Zambales and out of the province down to the plains of Central Luzon, north to Ilocos, and as far south as Manila, back to where it all started in the 1890s. Recognizable Katipunan names like Tomas Remigio, Restituto Javier and Aurelio Tolentino made noise again as they reorganized the Katipunan councils and rearmed the "brothers." The Katipunan was the idea that would animate the people and impel them, as it did to the followers of Padre Aglipay in Ilocos Norte, to their patriotic duty of resisting American occupation, against the collaborationist efforts of the *ilustrados* and *principales* who had banded themselves together as the *Partido Federalista.*

By the first quarter of 1900, the Katipunan influence had extended so far and wide that Aguinaldo, a fugitive in northern Luzon, had to sanction its existence officially by means of his own circulars. The man who had liquidated in 1897 the Katipunan idea and its founder, superseding them with his own person and republican concepts, was compelled in 1900 to accept the responsibility of bringing it back alive. And all because of the spark generated by San Miguel's work.

Had Aguinaldo erred, after all, in estimating his "man" in Zambales?

The *Presidente* had been wrong about his elite Kawit troops. In his flight to the north, these suspected assassins of Luna were among the first to desert the presidential party, though they themselves were the presidential *guards.* Aguinaldo had been wrong, too, about Daniel Tirona. This bosom friend and townmate who had caused much of the intrigues against Bonifacio in 1897 would surrender at Aparri without firing a single shot (though his forces were among the best armed, even with artillery pieces) even as his friend and chief was hurrying up north to join him in Isabela. The men who would stay by Aguinaldo's side and stick it out with him were neither of 1896 nor of Cavite. Goyo del Pilar, Manuel Tinio, Benito Natividad, Simeon Villa—these were names of another phase and setting of the Revolution. These were the true *republicanos:* schooled, patriotic, adventurous, and ambitious young men fighting for national independence, as well as for the good bourgeois life.

Surely enough, San Miguel was a veteran of 1896 and of Cavite. But was he not originally of the *Magdiwang* circle of revolutionaries who had an open or secret admiration for the *Supremo* more than the *Presidente*? True enough, San Miguel was dyed-in-the-wool *insurrecto*. But were there not two brands—one Katipunero, the other Republicano—of insurgencies all along? Was not San Miguel, in fact, resuming an inner revolution—the Katipunan's—that the Republic had always been careful to suppress? Had San Miguel served the Republic, and *not one man*, solely out of his pure conviction as a true Katipunero that (as he accepted in 1897) "our blood and our lives should be consecrated to no other purpose but the liberation of the mother country"? Or out of his firm belief that (as he exhorted in 1900) "the exclusive duty of brothers shall be . . . true unity and fraternity"?

Whatever his true sentiments and plans were, General San Miguel's Katipunan-based guerrilla warfare in Zambales was cut short not by the force of the invaders, but by the very "evils"—deceit, intrigue, factionalism, Cain killing Abel—he sought to "rectify."

Officially, Major-General Pantaleon Garcia had been appointed Commanding General of all Central Luzon provinces, with Brigadier-General Jose Alejandrino as his assistant. The Secretary of War, and therefore Lieutenant-General of the Army since Luna's death, was Ambrosio Flores. "Alleging that he was sick and had to bring his family to a safer place," said Alejandrino in his memoirs, Flores on his part named Alejandrino acting head of the war department. Alejandrino was also designated "chief of a column" whose mission it was to safeguard the artillery and ordnance pieces being evacuated in November 1899 to the Zambales Mountains. This column ceased to exist after it was alternately attacked and decimated by the American forces and by bolo bands believed by Alejandrino to be "Guardias de Honor." Alejandrino finally joined General San Miguel in northern Zambales, and he may have concurred (although he himself was an *ilustrado* who was never a member of the Katipunan) with the latter's plan to revive the secret society. It is even possible that circulars disseminated in January 1900, appearing to come from Secretary of War Flores and sanctioning the organization of the Katipunan society, were really drafted by Alejandrino (again possibly in collaboration with San Miguel) in the name of General Flores.

Internal trouble began when General Pantaleon Garcia came out of hiding to issue, on 9 January 1900, his own circular as

21

Commanding General of Central Luzon which negated the labors of General San Miguel. In this circular, written in the usual arrogant language of many generals of the Republic, Garcia announced the "official" list of guerrilla commanders recognized by his headquarters since 25 November 1899. Alejandrino was listed as commanding general for Pangasinan. But it was General Tomas Mascardo—not San Miguel—who was "officially" in command of Zambales (as well as Bataan), according to Garcia.

Pantaleon Garcia had been a leading *Magdalo* adherent in the "first war" and had taken part in the courtmartial and prosecution of the Bonifacio brothers. Did Garcia sense in the language of San Miguel's circulars, as well as in the person of the former *Bonifacista* himself, a potential "troublemaker" in the conduct of the republican struggle? Was Garcia acting upon orders from above to discredit San Miguel's work? Had he been influenced by other staunch *Aguinaldistas* like Mascardo?

San Miguel was in Iba, in central Zambales, when he began to sense foul moves from his own comrades in the Republic, which were obviously aimed at blocking his "katipunization" campaign. He learned that Major Alba of Mascardo's command was carrying out his guerrilla activities in a zone far beyond his own and which had already been designated for Lieutenant-Colonel Arce by San Miguel. On the 11th of January, San Miguel issued a memo letter to Major Alba and, for the first time, he affixed the words "Supreme Commanding General" to his full signature. And he reminded the meddlesome officer:

I entreat and request that you abstain [from meddling with Katipunan affairs] inasmuch as the local presidentes are able to do it, and you should devote yourself solely to attacking the enemy, if you wish . . .

Today more than ever the union of the province is needed, and I have sufficient personnel to prevent the province from becoming divided against itself, or some towns from declaring themselves independent from others. At the same time I also request that you issue [revoke?] orders to the towns where you have established the Katipunan in order to prevent disorders and unfavorable feeling toward us.

It is significant that San Miguel's sarcasm should be directed to a fellow officer in the republican army, and not to any of the "discontented" leaders. Although he himself would continue to fight as a general of the Republic, it is clear that San Miguel was a true

22

Katipunero pursuing true Katipunan goals. In the clash between 1896-1897 veterans (led by Aguinaldo) and 1898-1899 newcomers (led by Luna) San Miguel was naturally on the side of the former. But in that group there had always been former *Bonifacistas* like himself (and Ricarte) who had not quite forgotten their Katipunan roots.

That early in 1900, in fact, though still a fighter for the Republic, Luciano San Miguel was already championing—far ahead of Sakay and Malvar—the cause of the Katipunan.

Successor to Malvar

TIRED AND DISGUSTED, General San Miguel slipped out of Zambales back into home grounds in Cavite about the middle of March. Though he had become one of the "discontented" himself, this veteran of the wars of '96, '98 and '99 was still undaunted, was still full of fight. Luciano San Miguel was determined to fight it out against the Yanquis to the end.

He would sneer at his fellow generals who abandoned *Inang Bayan* and came in one by one to swear allegiance to America—*Magdalo* henchmen like Tirona, Garcia, and Pawa; and *ilustrado* opportunists like Flores, Canon, and Concepcion. And he would cheer for those brave and unbending "intransigentes"—Ricarte, Pio del Pilar, Hizon, and others—who would choose deportation to some faraway land rather than bend their knees to the American aggressors. He himself would not accept MacArthur's amnesty offer in June; instead he continued to fight in Cavite assisting Generals Trias and Noriel in their own guerrilla activities.

Aguinaldo was captured in March 1901. He hadn't fought to the death, nor had he chosen exile; instead, he called upon his generals to lay down their arms. "Enough of blood," Aguinaldo had said. And those words were echoed by Trias, then by Noriel, then by Malvar himself. But no such words could ever be heard among patriots and fighters crying out *"Mabuhay ang Bayang Tinubuan sa dugo at buhay ng Katipunan ng mga Anak ng Bayan!"*

In the natural line of succession in the revolutionary command, San Miguel found himself, after Malvar's surrender, when the war was supposed to have ended, nominally in charge not only of the whole of Cavite but of all existing "insurgent" affairs. He was the

23

next senior officer of the Republican forces qualified to succeed Malvar, and the only one now remaining in the field (the other being the Vibora still in exile).

Though he had been a republican general by choice, San Miguel had always been a Katipunan warrior at heart. Katipunan veterans around Manila knew this, just as they knew the republican leadership had once deposed San Miguel from his command in Zambales for his attempts to revive the Katipunan according to its original goals, and not in the "manner prescribed by the commanding general of Central Luzon." Back in Cavite, though he fought under Malvar, he continued to work for Katipunan objectives and for the fusion of factions.

On his part, San Miguel also knew, perhaps as a projection of his own sentiments, that many old followers of Bonifacio had merely dropped out of the Revolution out of loyalty to their *Supremo*. It was said that Emilio Jacinto was invited to occupy a post in Malolos in the days of *independencia*, but he declined. But this did not mean those veterans had accepted the American rule. This did not mean they were not aching to fight again. The 1898 experiment of Makabulos and his own experience in Zambales had proven well enough that those ignored and disenchanted veterans of the "first war" would forget past differences—if someone just came along to exhort them, unite them, and lead them.

Parallel to Malvar's organization, for example, another group outside the continuity of the republican struggle and one of purely Katipunan origins and membership was alive in Rizal, including Manila. In fact, documents attributed to this group were circulated as early as January 1901, about the same time the American military government began rounding up the "irreconcilables"—Mabini and Ricarte among them—for deportation to Guam. This group was apart from the "Junta de Amigos" of Katipunan veterans organized by Aurelio Tolentino for urban guerrilla actions in Manila, although there was certainly a link because of Tolentino himself who was one of the very few *ilustrado* Katipuneros. Even if Malvar, when he took over in April 1901, had heard of this group, it is doubtful that its leaders accepted his authority as supreme leader of the resistance forces.

By the time Taft's civil government took over in July from MacArthur's military command, this group had already become a force for the newly born Constabulary to reckon with. And by November, defying the Sedition Law, those "true members of the Katipunan and sons of *Katagalugan*" proceeded to draft the constitution that would give legitimacy to their new revolutionary government repudiating the fallen Republic. They ratified this constitution on Christmas Day of 1901 and then set up a "presidencia suprema" for that government, composed of Macario Sakay, Francisco Carreon, Domingo Moriones, Alejandro Santiago, Cenon Nicdao, Aguedo del Rosario, Nicolas Rivera, and others—all of them well-known *Bonifacistas* of the first revolution. If there was any link at all with the Malvar forces, this could have been possible only in the *Partido Nacionalista* that was formed in August, and only with personalities who had once belonged to the Bonifacio-Alvarez or Tondo-Noveleta or *Katagalugan-Magdiwang* alliance of 1896 Katipuneros.

This old Katipunan and the new Partido Nacionalista were in fact suspected by the American authorities as one and the same movement, particularly in its later stages, when the agitator Dr. Dominador Gomez was acting as its coordinator. General Henry T. Allen, then Chief of the Philippine Constabulary, stated in the *Annual Report of the Philippine Commission* for 1903:

> . . . Tagalog dramas of highly seditious nature were produced at first in Manila, subsequently in the provinces, under the auspices of said party . . . the ladrone bands of Cavite, Rizal and Bulacan were approached, and many were duly installed as members of the party. The labor union [*Union Obrera Democratica*], with the same president, Dr. Dominador Gomez, was also organized and practically united with the National[ist] party. The ladrone bands communicated with Manila through the local presidentes of this National[ist] party. A vigorous effort was made, but with only partial success, to have the Independent Filipino Church (Aglipayan movement) consolidate with these two organizations just mentioned. . . . Some of the old Katipuneros advocated the triple coalition, claiming that sentimental consideration for the triangular arrangement [of the Katipunan in its early pre-1896 stage] would appeal to the secret brotherhood that they hoped to resuscitate.

The Constabulary soon succeeded, however, in rounding up almost all of the leaders of the *Katagalugan* (Tondo) wing of the Partido that had initiated the new Katipunan government. Sakay and Nicdao were captured early in 1902—lucky for them because they would be included in the general amnesty of July 1902. But Moriones, Del Rosario, Rivera, and others who were caught after the amnesty period were given long terms in prison for "committing crimes after 1 May 1902."

Instead of surrendering to take advantage of the amnesty, the Katipunan government in hiding, now directed by Alejandro Santiago as "presidente supremo" in place of Sakay, activated its armed base. The guerrilla bands of Generals Julian Santos and Benito Santa Ana and Colonels Faustino Guillermo, Apolonio Samson, Ciriaco Contreras and Salustiano Cruz suddenly became active in Rizal and Bulacan. One source mentioned the involvement of these armed bands in the labor strikes earlier organized by Isabelo de los Reyes in Manila, for which he was arrested and jailed. While he was in prison in Malabon, the Katipunan leaders continued to communicate with De los Reyes.

On 7 July, P.C. Inspector Licerio Geronimo surprised and captured Domingo Moriones, "Minister of War," and Aguedo del Rosario, "Minister of Fomento," in a Katipunan meeting in Marikina. In retaliation, Colonels Guillermo and Samson placed Geronimo on their target list, tracked him down, and finally cornered him at Diliman on 15 July. Aguinaldo's ex-general was lucky to be able to escape, but Guillermo captured his constabulary uniform which he later used to trick and disarm the whole P.C. detachment of San Jose, Bulacan—in broad daylight.

In August, after the San Jose raid, Captain William Warren of the Bulacan Constabulary chased Guillermo and his raiders up to the Ipo mountains near Norzagaray. In a night encounter, Guillermo lost three men and five guns, but his men scored it by killing two *constabularios* and wounding four, including Captain Warren. By September, the entire Bulacan Constabulary, together with the "Bulacan Volunteers" made up of *principales* from the towns of Santa Maria and Obando, were after Faustino Guillermo and his guerrillas.

In Cavite, too, the guerrilla bands under San Miguel, Montalan, Felizardo, De Vega, and others had not surrendered with Noriel or Malvar in April, nor had they taken advantage of the amnesty in July. General San Miguel alone, among the generals not deported to Guam, "bore the distinction of never having taken the oath of allegiance"—in the words of Colonel William Scott, then commanding the Constabulary's First District. And revolutionaries outside of Cavite knew this, too.

On 1 October 1902, the Katipunan leadership gathered at one

of their mountain camps on the Rizal-Bulacan border. General Benito Santa Ana, as presiding officer, queried the assembly: "Are you all agreed that we proclaim General Luciano San Miguel as Captain-General, politico-military superior and general in chief of operations of these islands by reason of his seniority in field service?" The motion was seconded to a man and then the assembly drafted the document of appointment for San Miguel, signed by 13 movement leaders including Julian Santos, Apolonio Samson and others. But San Miguel had to be summoned yet from Cavite.

Meanwhile, Arturo Dancel (a notorious *federalista* who would be governor of Rizal in 1903) was authorized by the American civil government as mediator for the surrender of the "new Katipunan" forces in Rizal and Bulacan. The guerrillas were promised the same terms of the amnesty in July as long as the general surrender was made by 1 November 1902. Accordingly, Julian Santos, as lieutenant-general next in command to San Miguel, appeared to accept the compromise and the surrender was fixed at a place called Corral-na-Bato. Instead, on the last day of grace, Santos led the Katipuneros assembled there in an ambush operation that almost led to the massacre of a Constabulary detachment under Lieutenant J.J. Bates. Angered by this defiance, the entire Constabulary command in Rizal went out to hunt down General Santos and his "ladrones" for the remaining two months of 1902. When it was thought that Santos and his guerrillas would be hiding away in some remote jungle or mountain, he sent 80 of his riflemen to raid the town of Pasig on the night of 24 December, in what was to be remembered for years by Pasig townsfolk and by the Constabulary as the "Christmas Eve fireworks" of 1902.

It was also the eve, in a manner of speaking, of Luciano San Miguel's final and most glorious phase in his career as a revolutionary fighter. On 15 January 1903, unconsciously retracing Andres Bonifacio's footsteps in reverse, General San Miguel crossed over from Cavite to Rizal—and to his death.

Six years had passed since *Supremo* Andres Bonifacio made his own doomed trek to Cavite after he consented to personally lead the *Magdiwang*, one of two rival provincial councils of the Katipunan there. Within six months, the *Supremo* was a dead man—not from the bullets of the Spaniards, but at the hands of Emilio Aguinaldo's *Magdalo* henchmen.

Bonifacio's mistake was in taking sides in an intramural war

27

among Caviteños and then, having taken the side of *Magdiwang*, in trying to impose the policies of his own *Katagalugan* Council even on the *Magdalo* rebels. *Katagalugan* was, of course, the Katipunan of Tondo, as *Magdiwang* was the Katipunan of Noveleta and *Magdalo* the Katipunan of Kawit. It was the progenitor from which all the other Katipunan councils originated and it was, theoretically, the supreme council of the brotherhood—the *Junta Suprema*, the *Kataastaasang Kapulungan*, the *Haring Bayan*, or whatever it was called. Not two but three factions really fought out the internal war of the 1896 revolution in Cavite. And here, *Katagalugan*, in the persons of the Bonifacio brothers and their followers from Tondo (and, loosely speaking, the other Manileños who accompanied the *Supremo* to Cavite), became the proverbial outsider in the clan feud against which, in the end, the two Cavite factions would conspire. *Katagalugan* was eliminated.

In deciding the fate of Bonifacio among the *Magdiwangs*, Luciano San Miguel voted him out. He turned his back on the agitations of fellow *Magdiwang* generals for an open war with the *Magdalo*. And when the Bonifacio brothers were finally sentenced to death, San Miguel looked the other way. And yet, probably no one among the Katipuneros of *Magdiwang*, not even the Alvarezes or even Ricarte, embraced the sacred ideals of the Katipunan, heart and soul, more than Luciano San Miguel did. Perhaps it was because San Miguel, better than his *ilustrado-principalia* "brothers" in *Magdiwang*, could identify more with the plebeians who led that revolutionary society, for he himself was of common origins. Still, being Caviteño, his basic orientation was Cavite politics; being *provinciano*, his perception of the Katipunan ideology was never doctrinal, which was why, perhaps, he never really got along with the circle of original Katipunan ideologues (like Sakay and Carreon) who came from the cradle of *Katagalugan*.

San Miguel's "New Katipunan" in 1902-1903 was, truly enough, carried out in honest remembrance of the secret society according to its revolutionary teachings and practices, if not according to its revolutionary goals. Unity, brotherhood, the fusion of factions—this had always been Luciano San Miguel's single-minded preoccupation throughout his revolutionary career, from the *Magdiwang* days in Cavite to the second war of 1898, from the Central Luzon campaigns in 1899 to his 1900 guerrilla days in Zambales and Cavite. This, again, was what San Miguel sought to accomplish in coming to Rizal. Like the Bonifacio of 1896, San Miguel in 1903 would come to a region not his own to lead men in arms. But unlike Bonifacio, San Miguel would come not to divide the ranks of patriots, but to unite them.

From the angle of *Bonifacista-Aguinaldista* (or Katipunero-Republicano) politics, the capture of Emilio Aguinaldo in 1901 ended the leadership of the revolution of *Magdalo* as the *republica*. From the day the Katipunan was dissolved at Tejeros and the Bonifacio brothers were liquidated in 1897, the Revolution would entirely and solely be a *Magdalo* enterprise. If the Katipunan represented by the *Katagalugan* of Tondo went straight to its doom in Cavite, the *Magdalo* of Kawit "went places": to Biyak-na-Bato and Hongkong in 1897; to Malolos in 1898; to Cabanatuan, Tarlac, and Bayambang in 1899; to Lubuagan and Tierra Virgen in 1900; then, finally, to Palanan where it fell in 1901.

But *Magdalo* having fallen did not mean the end of the Revolution. In April 1901, a month after Aguinaldo's capture, Malvar took command. If this phase of the republican struggle was able to attract to its banner the plebeians and the peasants sworn to Katipunan ideals and goals, it was because Malvar had not been of *Magdalo*: he had been "neutral" in the internal wars of 1897 and if he ever took sides, he was more inclined to the *Supremo's* side. *Magdiwang* diehards would rally to his call in Cavite. And in August, there was an attempt of *Magdiwang* to reunite with *Katagalugan* in a new bid to lead the Revolution as they did in pre-*Magdalo* rule.

Magdiwang "turncoats" like Trias, Ricarte, San Miguel and even an Alvarez (Pascual) may have fought under the banner of *Magdalo* as the Republic—but not the Villanuevas, nor the Nocons, the Viratas, the Portillas, and certainly not the *Magdiwang* Generalissimo Santiago Alvarez. The remnants of *Magdiwang* headed by Alvarez and the survivors of *Katagalugan* headed by Sakay, together with other Katipunan veterans as well as new-generation revolutionaries of various persuasions—in short, the "left" of the Revolution—met that August of 1901 in what may be called the "Quiapo Assembly." Here was a gathering of *Bonifacistas* who may have been divided among themselves but who, on this occasion, united to bring about the birth of the original Partido Nacionalista.

As already stated, this was a unification of individua' movements and groups, outside of Malvar's. The *Katagalugan*

29

movement on its own proceeded to draft a constitution that would legitimize a projected revolutionary government repudiating the fallen Republic. Then they set up a "presidencia suprema" for their government with Sakay at its helm. But the *Katagalugan* movement's initial attempts to rise were retarded by Sakay's capture in January 1902. It was around this time, too, that full-scale operations began against Malvar in Batangas which ended with his surrender in April, after four months of hard fighting.

San Miguel had made his appearance not when Malvar or Sakay were in the field but when one had given up and the other had lain low. In fact, San Miguel appeared on the scene at a time when even the Partido Nacionalista was almost dead, its directors either in hiding or in prison. It was to save the revolutionary situation that Dr. Dominador Gomez as acting president of the Partido (representing the *obreros*) and Alejandro Santiago as acting "presidente supremo" of the *Katagalugan* government resorted to activating the "bastard" bands of Katipunan veterans that assembled in the Norzagaray mountains to elect San Miguel their overall leader.

And now in Rizal, as the new Generalissimo, Luciano San Miguel would provide a synthesis for the failed Republican and Katipunan armed struggles.

The San Miguelista Guerrillas

THE MORONG REGION was not new to Luciano San Miguel. A big part of it had comprised the Filipino Third Zone of Manila that he once commanded in 1898-1899. This zone had not been entirely broken up by the American forces, for after San Miguel abandoned his last lines of defense at San Francisco del Monte and followed the Filipino Army in its retreat to the north, Colonel Hermogenes (Mones) Bautista and his reserve force—mostly *sandatahanes* and mostly Katipunan veterans—stayed behind in the hills of Marikina and San Mateo. But although Bautista was San Miguel's second chief, the Third Zone was later reactivated not under his command but under General Licerio Geronimo.

Mones Bautista and Serio Geronimo were among the Katipunan generals named by Bonifacio in 1896 at the earliest stage of the Revolution. But while Bautista would later be relegated to a minor role and lesser rank (like Francisco de los Santos, Julian Santos,

Apolonio Samson, Faustino Guillermo, and other friends of Bonifacio), Licerio Geronimo managed to ingratiate himself with Aguinaldo, who stayed at his camp in Puray during the latter's escape from Cavite in June 1897, after Bonifacio's death. In the battle that took place there, Geronimo fought with great skill and drove off the Spanish forces with heavy losses. Because of that victory, says Ricarte in his memoirs, "the name of Licerio Geronimo was heard everywhere!"

Even the Spanish Governor-General heard of Geronimo. And when Admiral Dewey's U.S. fleet defeated the Spanish armada in Manila Bay in 1898, Geronimo was easily one of those named to command the Filipino Volunteer Militia against the Americans, along with such famous rebel commanders as Baldomero Aguinaldo, Mariano Trias, Artemio Ricarte, and Pio del Pilar. When Aguinaldo returned from exile shortly afterwards, all these militia commanders, with their arms and men, went to the side of the new Revolution—"except Licerio Geronimo who remained with Spain until the end," according to Taylor. This explains why Aguinaldo would appoint other chiefs (first Montenegro, then San Miguel) to command the Third Zone of Manila, although Geronimo would have been the most logical choice.

While Aguinaldo must surely have regretted Geronimo's seemingly unpatriotic act, yet he had not forgotten Geronimo's good work in the first revolution. And Aguinaldo was willing to give Geronimo a chance to redeem himself when he offered his services once more soon after the war with the Americans broke out. So, Aguinaldo designated his former savior at Puray the new chief of the Third Zone in place of then Colonel San Miguel—thus bypassing poor, ignored Mones Bautista, the ex-*Bonifacista*. The *Presidente* must surely have been elated on hearing of Geronimo's most famous exploit during that 1899 phase of the war—his successful defense of San Mateo against General Lawton's advance in December, resulting in the killing by his troops of that intrepid American general, the highest U.S. Army officer to lose his life in the entire Philippine campaign. This time, Geronimo's name was heard as far as the American continent!

Twice, in different wars, Licerio Geronimo made his name among his people. Then he let it fade into black legend. General Geronimo surrendered and swore allegiance to American rule in 1901, shortly after Aguinaldo did. When the American authorities, while the war still raged, began enlisting ex-officers of the "insurgent army" for their colonial force, the Philippine Constabulary, he was among its first recruits. By 1902, Lawton's once famous conqueror had fallen into ignominy as a mercenary Constabulary inspector hunted for liquidation by his former comrades in the Revolution.

If Serio Geronimo went over to the American side, the other senior officer of the Third Zone, Mones Bautista, did not. But neither did he want to fight anymore; all he wanted to do now was to go back to his farm in the foothills of Montalban. There, in those same mountains in 1896, seven "brothers" in the Katipunan vowed to fight and die for that brotherhood: Andres Bonifacio, Emilio Jacinto, Macario Sakay, Faustino Guillermo, Apolonio Samson, Francisco de los Santos, and Bautista himself. With Bonifacio and Jacinto dead, De los Santos deported to Guam, and Mones Bautista now holding a plow instead of his bolo, only three of the "brothers" were left to carry on that fight and fulfill that vow. But Sakay could not be located after he was amnestied in July. So, only Faustino Guillermo and Apolonio Samson would fight together with other Katipunan survivors in the army of General San Miguel.

While Geronimo and Bautista have had their biographies written, very scant and scattered materials can be found on the lives of such outlawed *insurrectos* as Samson and Guillermo. In Vic Hurley's book, Faustino Guillermo was the "jungle fox": the guerrilla genius behind the masterful bush warfare of the dreaded "Diliman Gang," as the Constabulary ridiculed his guerrilla band. Like many "original" Katipuneros, he had been unschooled; but one sees in the photograph taken after his capture (reproduced by Hurley in his book) the bearing of an intelligent, capable leader. Though he was not *taga*-Tondo, but a mere country yokel, Guillermo became prominent enough in the Bonifacio circle to be in its major meetings. While in Balara in 1896, Bonifacio named him one of the Katipunan generals, in command of San Francisco del Monte.(*) But his name disappears with Bonifacio's departure to

_____

(*)The others were Hermogenes Bautista for the whole of Morong (it was not renamed Rizal until 1901), Luis Malinis for Balara, Apolonio Samson for Novaliches, Cipriano Pacheco for Malabon Tambobong, Julian Santos for Marikina, and Licerio Geronimo for San Mateo.

his doom in Cavite. From here, we can only speculate on the activities of Faustino Guillermo.

It is possible that he remained in Balara. For the six months that Cavite was the battleground of the Revolution, Guillermo and the Morong rebels did nothing but sit and wait. The tragedy of the Katipunan in Morong was that after the Sons of the People had raised their cry of revolt against Spain, they had failed to become a real people's army. The bolos and bamboo spears were not replaced by guns and cannons, and the *sanggunians* did not transform into companies and battalions commanded by a hierarchy of officers in uniforms, as the *principalia*-led Katipunan in Cavite had become. Bonifacio the *Supremo* could not also be called, in a real sense, Bonifacio the Generalissimo—for the simple reason that he had no real army to speak of. When the Revolution returned to Morong in the middle of 1897, not the *Supremo* but the Generalissimo Emilio Aguinaldo was acclaimed leader of the Revolution—and not at Guillermo's camp in Balara, but at Licerio Geronimo's camp in Puray. In the assembly at Puray it is possible that Guillermo was there, too, although he was not among fellow *Katipuneros*— Pacheco, Bautista, De la Cruz, Geronimo and others—retained as generals of the Aguinaldo-led struggle. It is unlikely that he was at Biyak-na-Bato in subsequent months, for he was neither a signer of the Biyak-na-Bato constitution nor an officer of the "republic" set up there. But in one existing photograph of rebel leaders taken in Biyak-na-Bato, among those identified was a "Captain Guillermo"—could this be Faustino?

More questions: Was he involved in Jocson's subsequent uprising in 1898 in protest of the "truce" of Biyak-na-Bato? Was he among Katipunan veterans (Francisco Carreon, we know from his own account, was one of them) who would momentarily forget the *Supremo*'s fate and get carried away by the *independencia* fever of 1898? Did he gather men to participate in the siege of and attack on Manila? Was he among the "reserve troops" mobilized for the Third Zone of Manila? Did he fight the war against the Americans in the Geronimo Brigade or in the Pio del Pilar Brigade which later fought as guerrillas in the hills and jungles of Morong? Or did he enlist in the "Conquering Regiment of the Vibora" that Ricarte planned to capture Manila with in 1900? Or, like all true Katipuneros (like Jacinto and Sakay), did Faustino Guillermo simply drop out of the struggle and continue the work of spreading the Katipunan ideal right under the nose of the Republic?

The truth is, among the generals Bonifacio had appointed in 1896, only Geronimo and Pacheco had survived in the Army of the Republic. Some, like Mones Bautista, would play bit roles in the republican struggle as officers of the territorial militia. The rest, especially Guillermo and Samson, were not heard of—until after the Republic had crumbled with Aguinaldo's fall.

Apolonio Samson's name is more likely to pop out in a history quiz than Guillermo's. He was the peasant Katipunero in whose yard in Caloocan the Sons of the People first gathered on the eve of the Revolution. Prior to this, as chairman of the Katipunan *Karitas* chapter of Novaliches, he had attended meetings presided by the *Supremo*. According to Pio del Pilar in his autobiography, Samson led the bolomen from Novaliches who joined Bonifacio's attack on San Juan del Monte on 30 August 1896. Like all the rest, they were later scattered. Samson reunited with Bonifacio in the woods of San Francisco del Monte, and then followed him to Balara. In that camp, the *Supremo* named Apolonio Samson one of his generals.

He was among the "men from Balara" in the Bonifacio party dominated by the "men of Katagalugan" (Tondo) that the *Supremo* brought along with him to Cavite. Ricarte saw him there and names him (together with Francisco Carreon, Alejandro Santiago, and others) among those arrested and tried with the *Supremo* for the crime of sedition in April 1897. Although the *Supremo* was executed, the lives of his disciples were spared; but they, especially Samson, would have no part of the Aguinaldo-led revolution. In the second war of 1898 and in the anti-American war of 1899—the republican phase of the struggle—Apolonio Samson was nowhere to be seen or heard. Then suddenly, in 1902, he was the "terror" of Novaliches to the Constabulary. In the Constabulary records, his family name was spelled "Sampson."

Let us not forget Julian Santos. There were two Julians in Marikina who became Katipunan generals in 1896. Julian de la Cruz is hardly known to students of the Revolution: what we know about him is that he later recognized Aguinaldo's leadership, signed the Biyak-na-Bato constitution, and on returning to Marikina was assassinated allegedly by minor *Aguinaldistas* jealous of his position, in another sad case of "*kapatid laban sa kapatid.*" The more famous Julian was Julian Santos y Flores, probably of the expansive Santos clan of Marikina whom Ricarte in his memoirs mistook for the

Julian murdered by fellow *insurrectos*. Unlike De la Cruz who turned *republicano*, Santos was forever *Bonifacista*. A third Julian was the notorious *guardia civil*, Julian Paguia, who became a colonel in the Pio del Pilar Brigade. In a confrontation with the men of Julian Santos at Barangka after the San Juan fiasco in 1896, a patriot hacked the Civil Guard's face with his bolo, leaving an ugly scar that would forever remind Julian Paguia of his days of infamy. All three Julians were controversial figures who led tragic lives. General Julian Santos, after his capture, was sentenced to death by hanging. But as the Constabulary had officially put it, he "cheated the gallows." He died in prison.

Humble men of the likes of Santos, Samson, and Guillermo made up the core of the San Miguelista guerrillas. They were unschooled *ignorantes* compared to the "college-boy" generals of the Republic. They were inarticulate *taga-bukid* compared to the "city-boy" ideologues of *Katagalugan*. But they, too, were men of strong convictions—Katipuneros of undoubted faith, fighters of unwavering patriotism. And for these holdouts of 1902-1903, one cannot help remembering those appropriate lines by Isabelo de los Reyes: "Among them there was not a single rich man, nor one of a learned profession, and they began, led by just common sense which has so many times shown itself in the people, to be more desirable than the wisdom of intellectual pretenders."

Constabulary authorities believed that the organization led by General San Miguel was the "most formidable band of 'patriotic' outlaws the Constabulary has had to cope with." The Chief of Constabulary himself, General Allen, considered the outbreak the San Miguelistas caused in Rizal-Bulacan as the "most serious disturbance, amounting to a local uprising."

An uprising it was all right, but was it merely local?

Agitations were about this time simultaneously developing in nearby provinces, particularly those in the north where San Miguel had fought as a soldier of the Republic. And the personalities involved had one time or another worked with San Miguel. In Zambales, where San Miguel had commanded republican guerrillas before he was deposed by the "insurgent high command," seven northern towns of that province threatened to revolt. Their leader was Roman Manalang, who had been San Miguel's executive officer in the Zambales Battalion and who, like San Miguel, never swore allegiance to the United States. Manalang was among the generals named by Makabulos in 1898 whom Aguinaldo deposed but later reinstated with the rank of lieutenant-colonel. Another deposed 1898 general, Gregorio Gonzales, the liberator of southern Zambales from Spanish rule, had in 1902 reappeared in Bataan commanding a column of guerrillas classified, of course, as "bandits" by the Constabulary. In Mexico, Pampanga, where the San Miguel Brigade fought many battles, a Manila-directed conspiracy was bared involving old frontline *compañeros* of San Miguel—among them Modesto Joaquin, Felix Galura and Manuel Ruiz (yes, the same Ruiz who would later work with Ricarte in Hong Kong). And in Cavite at this time, the irregular armies of Montalan and Felizardo, who would later provide the armed base for Sakay's own movement, certainly considered themselves part of San Miguel's command as they had been in Malvar's time.

Whatever influence San Miguel wielded on these personalities in those provinces, his own activity in Rizal-Bulacan had by itself reached alarming proportions. Says Vic Hurley: "On several occasions he had surprised and destroyed detachments of Constabulary and his forces had grown to a well-disciplined and well-armed army."

Two examples where the *constabularios* were "soundly whipped" (Hurley's words) by San Miguel's guerrillas were the attacks made on Captain Warren's unit that January of 1903 and on Lieutenant H.R. Twilley's the following February after San Miguel's appearance. Both actions had taken place in Bulacan province under the directions of Colonels Guillermo and Contreras.

The disturbances caused by General San Miguel's initial guerrilla raids were such that "the month of February found every available Constabulary soldier in the Rizal-Bulacan area in the field in an attempt to locate San Miguel and destroy his force"— according to Hurley. The Native Scouts in Caloocan—Lieutenant Nickersen's First Macabebes and Lieutenant Neff's Twenty-first Ilocanos—were directed to assist in the Constabulary operations. A posse of "civilian volunteers" from Obando, organized and led by one Teodoro Donato, also joined the hunt. Then they changed their minds, deserted their leader, and went over en masse to San Miguel's side.

As a rule, except for "Ampil's Volunteers" in Cainta, the municipal police forces in the Rizal and Bulacan towns affected by San Miguel's operations were considered worthless by the

Constabulary authorities. As one report summed up their impotence: "Work accomplished by municipal police was scarcely nothing." There was even reason for the Constabulary to suspect that these police forces were secretly in cahoots with the "outlaws," if they were not guerrillas themselves. The telling fact is that in Rizal province alone, an aggregate of 94 firearms assigned to the *policia*—30 Remington rifles, 13 shotguns, 51 revolvers—were reported "lost" for 1903. The Constabulary hinted that this could have resulted from San Miguel's edict that "any municipal police or Constabulary who gave up their arms without resistance [during confrontation] would be released."

In the short time that San Miguel took charge of "insurgent" affairs, it seemed, indeed, that the factions had come together at last in a common struggle. Sadly, though, this was not true. At the time the two leading *Bonifacistas*, Macario Sakay and Francisco Carreon, who had revived the *Katagalugan* council of Tondo as a separate movement, were nowhere to lend a helping hand. And even the *Magdiwang* wing of the Partido Nacionalista (represented by Santiago Alvarez)—now that San Miguel was in the field—stood by and did nothing. The only men who rode with San Miguel were the Katipunan veterans of Rizal and Bulacan who elected him their chief—those unaligned peasant armed bands outside *Katagalugan* and *Magdiwang*. Of the *Katagalugan* leaders only Alejandro Santiago was known to have cast his lot with the San Miguelistas, but perhaps only because Sakay himself had not made his appearance and because Samson (his companion in Cavite in 1897) and Guillermo were also his close friends.

General Julian Santos, second in command, and Colonel Apolonio Samson were active all this time on the Rizal side of San Miguel's command. Their forces operated mostly around the Marikina River valley, where San Miguel himself often stayed. Most of the time they set up their headquarters at that isolated (and now extinct) spot in Marikina called Corral-na-Bato, where an old stone fort lay hidden among the brush along a tributary of the Marikina River. From this base, during February 1903, San Miguel and Santos made a series of raids through Cainta, Taytay, Antipolo and Boso-boso.

On 7 February, Colonel Cary Crockett, a descendant of the legendary Davy and then a captain commanding the crack Manila Company of the Constabulary, encountered San Miguel and his men at Boso-boso. The night previous to this fight, Crockett had received these orders from General Allen:

San Miguel reported in vicinity of Bobosco [sic]. Costello's force of Scouts [23rd Ilocanos, stationed at San Mateo] is ordered across the mountains and should reach Bobosco tomorrow. A mixed force of Scouts and Constabulary are moving out from Pasig via Antipolo to arrive at Bobosco same time. Your company will proceed at once to strike Bobosco from the north and cooperate with other columns.

Crockett took his Manila P.C. Company to Boso-boso as ordered and entered the town to find the *presidente* with his head "bound with a bloody rag." Crockett was told how San Miguel came to Boso-boso the previous day and ordered his men to cut off the *presidente*'s ears as punishment for being an *americanista* (a slight sentence compared to Sakay's later death penalty on the same *presidente*). Then the guerrillas left and were now strongly entrenched on the other side of the Boso-boso River, waiting for an assault. From the church tower, Vic Hurley narrates, Crockett could see through his field glasses the "strong position of the insurgents." But he noticed a thick jungle on San Miguel's right which would cover a flank movement. At dawn of the 8th, without waiting for any of the hunting parties, Crockett attacked the "bandits" from the rear of their trenches, hoping they would be caught unawares. Crockett moved his men so close he had a clear view of the "blue shirts and red blanket rolls of the troopers of San Miguel." But the wily San Miguel, a veteran of bush warfare, saw through Crockett's stratagem. Skillfully he withdrew his troops and eluded his would-be captor.

After this Boso-boso encounter, the senior Constabulary inspector of Rizal, Captain Ira Keithley, fielded a considerable force under four officers (one of them Lieutenant Licerio Geronimo) to track down the guerrillas. General San Miguel lured his pursuers to Corral-na-Bato. Here, on 9 February, the San Miguelistas almost had the government troops trapped in a bloody fight that lasted for almost two hours. One of the American officers commanding the native mercenaries, Lieutenant Harris, whom Hurley described as "a young and very blond Georgian," was killed by the Katipunan fighters at the beginning of his military career.

San Miguel did not leave his Corral-na-Bato. And early in March, his guerrillas fought a company of Macabebe mercenaries who suddenly attacked their camp and forced them to retreat with several losses. General Julian Santos was chased through all of Diliman into the thickly wooded country of San Francisco del Monte. Efforts to surround him there initially failed. Finally, 400 scouts and 200 *constabularios* formed a cordon and pushed the guerrillas toward the Pasig River where they were either rounded up or killed. Santos again miraculously escaped this dragnet, but his *anting-anting* finally failed him when he was captured while hiding in Navotas about the middle of March.

Although Guillermo, Samson, Contreras and their men were still active, the end was coming near for Luciano San Miguel.

Death at Corral-na-Bato

CORRAL-NA-BATO had "a fatal fascination for San Miguel," a bewildered Vic Hurley writes in *Jungle Patrol*. True. In spite of his two previous fights in that place, San Miguel gathered his army there again for another battle on 27 March. This time, two companies of Macabebes fought him.

Let us hear from Hurley again:

Early in the morning, the force under Lieutenant Nickersen was moving cautiously along the banks of the San Francisco River when the advance point contacted the force of San Miguel in a region that was densely studded with towering bamboo. The outlaws gave way and the scout force moved in a circular flank motion which encompassed the band.

The voice of San Miguel was heard as he discovered this enveloping movement. There was a patter in the long grass and the sound of a few desultory shots. When the point again made contact with the insurgents, it was to find them at refuge behind the stone walls of an old fort. This fortress, built at a bend of the San Francisco River, was composed of but two walls—the other two sides were protected by the river itself.

It was a formidable position. . . .

This third Battle of Corral-na-Bato proved to be General San Miguel's last, and probably best, exploit. Here was fought what may be regarded the last great battle of the Philippine anti-American resistance in Luzon.

To the Americans this battle proved once again what their native recruits were capable of when given proper equipment and leadership. The Macabebes assaulted the "insurrecto" positions with fixed bayonets and San Miguel and his fighters waited with their bolos ("brother subjugating his own brother"—had these thoughts flashed through in San Miguel's mind?). When the battle finally began it was hand-to-hand and it was a spirited combat, brutal and gory, that ended with so many casualties on both sides. The river banks of Corral-na-Bato turned pink with the blood of Filipinos fighting one another to achieve *freedom* in each own's broadest, or most limited, concepts.

One of the Americans commanding the Scouts, Lieutenant Reese, who fought with much gallantry, was among those seriously wounded. But the "insurrectos" suffered a greater loss: when the smoke of battle had cleared away, there lay their hero General Luciano San Miguel among the dead. A stray Krag bullet had earlier hit the Filipino leader; seeing him bleeding, his guerrillas started to fall back in an attempt to carry away their wounded commander.

Here's how Vic Hurley dramatically viewed the Generalissimo's last few moments:

As the enemy retreated across the river, Lieutenant Nickersen rallied fifteen of his men and crossed in pursuit. His attention was directed almost immediately to several men leading an officer who appeared to be wounded. Nickersen directed his fire at this group. At the first shot from his pistol, one of the group dropped; the rest broke for the brush, leaving the wounded man to make his way alone.

A Sergeant from the 4th Scout Company raised his rifle and advanced upon the weary figure that weaved there groggily in the bright sunlight. The wounded insurgent raised his revolver and fired one wavering shot. . . . A split second later came the retaliatory shot from the rifle of the Sergeant, and General San Miguel pitched forward, shot through the head.

Henry Parker Willis in 1905, writing his "study on American colonial policy," hints at Macabebe barbarism with a rueful comment on San Miguel's death—how "it was necessary to summon outsiders before San Miguel could be recognized among the dead, there being not a solitary member of his band who was not either dead or so seriously wounded as to be incapable of rational speech."

And William Henry Scott, writing 80 years later on responses to that colonialism, retells how that very night, in fact, while Luciano San Miguel's body lay unburied where it fell, "his victors feasted and danced in Macabebe." Scott then recounts how the nationalist paper *Los Obreros* editorially "expressed . . . an outrage . . . probably shared with many Filipinos"—in his own

40

retranslation of a Supreme Court record in the case against the paper's editor, Dominador Gomez:

> A victory would have been better crowned by burying with sincere sorrow the corpses of those who died fighting, uttering ardent and fervent prayers for their eternal rest. If the baptism with sacred water blots out original sin, the red baptism with one's own blood—that martyrdom which is sealed with the last sigh—also washes away crimes and wickedness from the innocent remains of a corpse, in the presence of which Nemesis herself, with all the inexorable vengeance of the sword, considers herself fully revenged and satisfied.

Thus died the luckless Luciano San Miguel. Like Bonifacio, he went to his doom beyond his own native place. Like Bonifacio, he died without finishing his work. Like Bonifacio, he died at the hands of his own countrymen—in this case, the Macabebe mercenaries—in a recurring scene of brother killing another brother. But unlike Bonifacio, San Miguel's was a true hero's death. He had fought against the invader to the last drop of his blood until, as Hurley pictured it, he "lay huddled beneath a bamboo clump with a bullet through his brain."

Truly, he had consecrated his blood and his life for the *kalayaan ng Inang Bayan.*

Two important papers were found in Luciano San Miguel's pockets. One was the document appointing him to command the resistance forces. The other was a calling card from Apolinario Mabini.

John Bancroft Devins, editor of the *New York Observer*, had in 1905 written *An Observer in the Philippines* where he devotes a number of pages on the Mabini-San Miguel incident. In this book, Devins translates and reproduces the full texts of two pertinent Mabini letters—one addressed to General San Miguel and the other to the American civil governor, William Howard Taft.

Mabini had returned from exile and took the oath of allegiance to the American government late in February 1903. It appears that San Miguel, through the underground, shortly after, greeted Mabini in the name of the movement and sought his advice. Mabini, though born of the masses, had not been a Katipunero; but he had been leader of the nationalist party in the *republica* that advocated independence and nothing else, and to which San Miguel had certainly once belonged. On a visiting card Mabini replied to the *guerrillero* with a short note, Devins says, "that he had not been long enough in the islands to answer, but that he would write a letter." Mabini's card was later recovered from San Miguel's dead body.

On being shown Mabini's card taken from the guerrilla hero at Corral-na-Bato, Governor Taft, notes Devins, "expressed surprise that so soon after taking the oath of allegiance Mabini should open communications with men in arms against the government." Mabini's reply to this was contained in his letter to Taft, dated 9 April 1903. In it, Mabini tells the American governor (in Devins' English) that he really sent the card in response to San Miguel's "greetings of welcome and requesting my opinion in regard to his attitude"—that is, as a holdout against America—and that weeks later he wrote him a letter "in which I endeavored to proved that armed contention is ruinous to the country."

Mabini, as Devins quotes him, counseled his former colleague in the Republic with these words:

Since you ask me my opinion concerning your action, I will clearly inform you in accordance with my method of thinking.

I do not consider that the liberty enjoyed today in this archipelago can be followed by independence through means of arms at the present time. The people do not move because they have no arms, and even if they had them they would have nothing to eat. Although you might find another nation that would like to furnish arms and supplies, this nation also would like to annex this territory, and if this should happen our misfortune would still be greater.

If we should proceed gradually, as, in fact, you are doing, the war would continue and possibly our nation would never enjoy prosperity, because the war would finally turn into a poisonous disease which would greatly increase our weakness. *Understand well that we are now killing each other.*

The underscoring is supplied to emphasize a point that Luciano San Miguel, reading the letter, would have underlined himself. The letter itself might have indeed appealed to San Miguel, for it contained honest words of counsel from a true friend and countryman. More from Mabini:

It seems to me that at the present time we should endeavor to secure independence through the paths of peace. Let us cease [the armed struggle] that the people may rest, that it may work to recover from its recent proprietary losses. Let us conform to the opinion of the majority, although we may recognize that by this method we do not obtain our desires. This is, I believe, the surest and most fit method of obtaining the welfare of all.

Let us deliberate and hold an assembly to treat of these matters. In case you are in conformity with this and return to peace, determine upon the necessary conditions that you should ask in order to save yourselves from any vexations, and if you think that I should transmit your petition to the constituted authorities I am disposed to comply at any time.

There are those who say your procedure is the cause of many abuses and methods which are unfavorable to the country, but I believe that the remedy for this, if true, is not comparable to the great poverty which would be born of a war apparently interminable. I believe that as long as the Filipinos do not endeavor to liberate themselves from their bonds the period of their liberty will not arrive.

Excuse me for telling you this. If, perchance, you are not in accord with my opinion, this will not, as far as I am concerned, be a motive for destroying our former friendship and companionship. Order your humble servant whenever you see fit.

Coming as it was from the "brains" of the ill-fated Republic, Mabini's "peace" missive might have prevented, at least, the tragedy at Corral-na-Bato. But the letter was dated 27 March 1903 on the same day San Miguel was killed—it never reached his hands.

Mabini would say in his aforementioned note to Taft that San Miguel's courier came back to him the next day saying the letter "had not reached the hands of San Miguel . . . but had been delivered to another officer of the band." Mabini further told Mr. Taft:

I have just been informed that the letter is in the possession of Faustino Guillermo, chief of the band, who, with his people, is disposed, so they say, to follow the counsels given in the said letter. But there exists another and larger band, under the command of Alejandro Santiago and Apolonio Samson; this Alejandro Santiago is, according to reports, the successor of San Miguel. Those chieftains have not received the letter yet, for the reason that the frequent expeditions and patrols of the Constabulary render communication very difficult; no one dares to search for them, for fear of falling into the hands of the officers of public order. They tell me that it is necessary that the persecution should not be so active, if only for a few days, for them to secure an opportunity to hold intercourse; or that a safe-conduct pass should be furnished them, so they can send a person to look for them and deliver the letter.

I must confess frankly that the late San Miguel was an old acquaintance and even friend of mine; but the chiefs above mentioned I do not know personally, and I am not acquainted with their antecedents. . . .

We know Mabini died shortly after in May. He hadn't lived long enough to see Faustino Guillermo and Alejandro Santiago fall into the hands of the Constabulary in June. "We gave up hope after the General's death," Guillermo told his captors, "and our only resort was to hide." Hide they did farther into the mountains with some friends, or so they thought until they realized too late they were victims of a ruse: their "friends" turned out to be *secretas* of the Constabulary. We'll never know if Mabini, had he lived longer, would have done anything to at least save Guillermo (whom he did not know "personally") from hanging in Pasig a year later. Santiago was meted out a long prison term for rebellion. Apolonio Samson was never heard from again, though his house in Kangkong would become a Katipunan shrine and a busy Caloocan street would be named in remembrance of him—as the Katipunero of 1896, not as the outlaw terror of 1902.

Caloocan is perhaps the only place that honors Luciano San Miguel with a street, too, as a general of the Republic. But such an honor is too small for the stature of the man who had labored greatly and even *gave his life* for the *Inang Bayan*.

San Miguel alive (notwithstanding his name) was no saint, in the pious meaning of the word. But San Miguel killed and baptized in his own blood at the Battle of Corral-na-Bato must be the Saint of the Intransigent, for he was as uncompromising as that worthy namesake of more than a thousand years back, St. Lucian of Antioch, unsurrendered martyr in the name of Christ. He was both a hero and a martyr because, having fallen heroically in battle, American propaganda killed him a second time, in a manner of speaking, in the minds of his countrymen. Thus, in "official history," where Tirad Pass became a shrine, Corral-na-Bato was a mere bandit's grave buried in oblivion.

Yet, Luciano San Miguel was one of the greatest, if belittled, fighters who ever fought in our past wars for national independence. There is no doubt that he was a good patriot--a "sincere insurrecto," as Hurley would put it. He and Gregorio del Pilar were the only generals of the Republic to die in action in the Philippine-American War. But while the hero of Tirad Pass sacrificed his life for "mi Presidente," the hero of Corral-na-Bato sacrificed his own for the people. He and Artemio Ricarte were the true "irreconcilables"—fighters to the last, "insurrectos" until their deaths. But while Ricarte never gave up his convictions in prolonged exile and incarceration, San Miguel fought for his own unto death in the field of battle. For having died so gloriously, in fact, San Miguel became Ricarte's own personal hero and inspiration in his own heroic but futile attempts to continue the Revolution.

Vic Hurley thinks General San Miguel's resistance movement was really the last scene—not Malvar's—in the "respectable phase" of the Philippine-American War. "With the passing of San Miguel," he says, "the final heartbeat of the Philippine Insurrection sounded." Hurley thinks the legitimate leadership of the Revolution ended with General San Miguel, too. He continues: "His death was followed by the surrender of many minor leaders, and never again was the United States to encounter resistance from any legitimate leader."

But Hurley thinks wrong. If San Miguel was "legitimate" because he fought as a general of the Republic, so would Sakay be who preceded him in the Katipunan and never deviated from the "correct path" of its armed struggle (and which San Miguel himself followed in 1903), and so would the various officers be of the Republic or the Katipunan who (following San Miguel's example) later consolidated under Sakay's leadership to keep the anti-American resistance alive, and so would the unconquered Vibora be in spite of the fruitlessness of his constant efforts to raise an army with which to liberate his country from—to use his own words—"the American and Filipino imperialists."

It is true that Malvar was the last general of the Republic to *surrender*. It is also true that Luciano San Miguel was the first of the *unsurrendered* patriots to die fighting for *Independencia*. But nobody even knows that an authentic revolutionary hero died fighting at Corral-na-Bato. Nobody even knows that there was a Corral-na-Bato.

There were no tears shed, no hymns sung, no monuments built by next-generation Filipinos for San Luciano San Miguel.

2

CAVITE'S
PEASANT HERO

SHATTERING THE MYTH
OF JULIAN MONTALAN
AS BANDIT AND SCAMP

two:

CAVITE'S PEASANT HERO

Magdiwang's Revolucionario

JULIAN MONTALAN was, to begin with, *makabayan*—and not the vicious "ladrone" most Filipinos had always known him to be since early American "empire days." He was a true revolutionary fighter, a veteran of the Cavite revolution of 1896 who fought on to the second war of 1898, on to the "respectable" anti-American resistance of Aguinaldo and Malvar (1899-1902), and on to the so-called "bandit phase" of the so-called "Philippine Insurrection" led by San Miguel and Sakay (1903-1907).

Here was an honest-to-goodness *taga-bukid* who never learned how to read and write (he signed his court records in 1906 with an "X" mark) but, for ten long years, never ceased fighting for his country's *independencia*—however he might have perceived that ideal—and then suffered imprisonment/exile for an even longer time for persisting as a holdout for *Inang Bayan.*

Though illiterate, he had charisma, which led one American colonial writer, Vic Hurley, to comment that Montalan's "renown among the natives was not measurable." And whether the American accusation that he was a "criminal from boyhood" was true or false, he was in his heyday, at least in his native Cavite, the hero of the peasantry. The charismatic Montalan—long hair, *anting-anting*, folk legend and all—was indeed the true representation of the rude and unschooled but consistently revolutionary peasant who fought in *all* phases of the Revolution.

In those early years of the Empire, intransigents in the hands of the Americans were either hanged or deported or left to rot in the *bartolinas* of the old Bilibid. Montalan was one of the few who remained elusive, who chose to stay in the mountains and refused to be "benevolently assimilated" by swearing allegiance to the United States after Malvar surrendered in 1902. For this reason, the American authorities in the Philippines naturally ranked him high among Filipino "bad guys" pictured in their "WANTED" posters, carrying a few thousand pesos reward (a fortune in those days) on their heads.

Since then, the veteran revolutionary fighter from San Francisco de Malabon was consigned to historical ignominy and reduced, at best, into one more Cavite legend. To the *americanos* and their *americanistas,* he was nothing more than an ornery, bloodthirsty, murdering highway robber who preyed upon his own people under the "convenient cloak of patriotism." But to the Cavite masses of that first half-decade of American occupation, he was the romantic folk hero idolized by his class all over the world through the ages—an Emiliano Zapata of a different clime leading Tagalog peons against the tyranny of both *hacendero* and *estrangero,* a Robin Hood of the Philippine forests taking from the moneyed landlords to share with the have-nots, an *eastern* Frank James raiding government convoys and installations, or, right at home in Cavite, another Casimiro Camerino risen from the 1860s and living as an outlaw for reason and justice.

As time went by, Filipino children of the 1900s grew up reading history textbooks written by American authors like David Barrows, who would propagate such myths as "the most desperate and cruel leaders in the history of the insurrection" of such worthless scamps as "Montalon" (Barrows, Taylor, Blount, Hurley and all the others never did learn to spell his name correctly!). So, it was this dark legend of Montalan as the bandit terror of the 1900s that prevailed in colonial minds; it was such historical lies as this one that we were made to "swallow hook, line and sinker"—to put it in Yanqui terms—for so many years. And it took a resurgence of nationalism in the 1960s, six decades after, for Filipino historians and students of history to reinvestigate and reevaluate the true worth of such outcasts of history as Julian Montalan, as well as the true character of their belittled resistance movements against American imperialist aggression.

"Official history, influenced by colonial scholarship, has presented the struggle against the Americans as a short one," the nationalist historian Renato Constantino made it clear to us in the

1970s. His lament: "It has honored the collaborators and all but ignored the resistance of the people."

The resistance Constantino talks about was the Katipunan-led and peasant-based armed struggle that went on, astonishing and riling the Americans, after the *ilustrado* revolution ended with the surrender of Malvar. Those were the suppressed years of the Philippine anti-American resistance—what was derisively called the "ladrone" period in American accounts—when "bands of outlaws, criminals and irresponsibles" (to use the language of Governor-General Smith in 1907) still held out in the hills of Cavite, Laguna, and Batangas, not to mention Rizal, Bulacan, Pampanga, the Bicol region, Leyte, Samar, Negros, and the Moro provinces. Those hold-outs offered armed resistance to the Philippine Constabulary and Philippine Scouts enlisted, clothed, fed, drilled, and paid to subjugate their fellow Filipinos. And they made guerrilla raids upon the towns—the only areas really under American occupation—to punish the pro-American *principales* and *ilustrados* who had accommodated themselves into American-sponsored civil service.

The same "official history" that glorified surrender (like Malvar as "last general to surrender") and collaboration (like Arellano as "first chief justice of the supreme court"), Constantino again deplores, "has paid scant attention to the real heroes who continued to keep faith with the people and with the original goals of the Katipunan."

Julian Montalan was probably not a Katipunero in the exact meaning of the word, as one would apply it to an Emilio Jacinto, or to a Macario Sakay. But he was certainly one of the first revolutionaries of Cavite to respond to the Katipunan armed struggle for national independence against the colonial rule of Spain. He was among the first volunteers of San Francisco de Malabon (now General Trias) who rose from the ranks of *Magdiwang*, one of two provincial councils of the Katipunan in Cavite and the one with closer sympathies to Andres Bonifacio's own *Katagalugan* supreme council of Tondo.

General Artemio Ricarte, writing his memoirs in prison in 1904, remembered Montalan as one of the "daring youths" of San Francisco de Malabon who, between late September and early October of 1896, launched a series of bold (though costly) attacks on the well-fortified Spanish positions at Caridad. When Ricarte cites him again, young Montalan is already a captain in the rebel

51

forces of General Mariano Trias (the man after whom San Francisco de Malabon was later renamed).

When the *Magdiwang* joined hands with the rival faction, *Magdalo*, in February 1897, to defend Bacoor, where the *ilustrado* General Edilberto Evangelista heroically fell, Montalan fought so well against the Spaniards, displaying exceptional courage and skill, that he was promoted after the battle to the rank of commander. Emilio Aguinaldo himself, writing his own reminiscences in old age, could still single out Montalan in this particular battle. *"Dito ko namalas at napuri ang katapangan ni Komandante Julian Montalan!"*—the Old Warrior from Kawit interjects his recollection of Major Montalan's brave act. But Montalan's conduct was even more impressive during the *Magdiwang*'s own victorious defense of San Francisco de Malabon in March. Commanding one of General Luciano San Miguel's battalions, Julian Montalan emerged from that hard-won battle a living hero—and a lieutenant-colonel.

Montalan's fame among the Cavite provincial folks was so widespread, even the *Magdalo* rebels themselves held him in awed respect. This was proven true when the *Magdalo* forces under Colonels Bonzon and Pawa were sent to arrest Andres Bonifacio in Limbon, a barrio of Indang, after that mess in Tejeros. The *Magdalo* men would hesitate at first when they learned of the presence of Montalan's forces near Limbon. Montalan, though a Caviteño himself, had been known as a Bonifacio admirer; after all, he was of *Magdiwang*, the group that was for a time friendly with the *Supremo*, besides sharing a common lowly origin with the plebeians from Tondo. Only after Montalan brought away his forces from Limbon to join the fight (against the Spaniards) at Indang did Bonzon and Pawa proceed to Limbon the very next day to carry out their grim mission.

Later, during the early American period, an older Montalan would become notorious as an outlaw—that is, a guerrilla holdout outlawed by the Bandolerismo Act of 1902 which was passed by the U.S. Philippine Commission, as Ricarte said (in a letter to Jose P. Santos in 1930, quoted in Antonio Abad's book on Sakay), "in order that those patriots who refused to surrender [after the 1902 amnesty] might be prosecuted as outlaws." In other words, the Bandolerismo Act was a repressive measure against the doomed but continuing nationalist, anti-federalist, anti-imperialist struggle that Montalan had elected to take part in. For doing so, Julian

Montalan the *Makabayan* was himself a doomed man. As Article 1 of this Act ordained:

> Whenever three or more persons conspiring together shall form a band of robbers for the purpose of stealing carabaos, cattle, horses, rice or personal property of any description, or for the purpose of abducting persons either for the purpose of extortion or obtaining ransom, or for any other purpose by means of force or violence, and shall be armed with deadly weapons for this purpose, they shall be deemed highway robbers or brigands, and every person engaged in the original formation of the band, or joining thereafter, shall, upon conviction thereof, be punished by death or imprisonment for not less than twenty years, in the discretion of the court.

Had the Bandolerismo Act been passed in 1901, Aguinaldo, Trias, Malvar, Lukban and all those "respectable" generals of the Republic would have been outlawed and condemned under its provisions, too. Julian Montalan had been in the thick of that *ilustrado*-led war against the Americans as a colonel of republican forces under Generals Trias, Ricarte, and Noriel. But he refused to surrender with Trias in March 1901, nor with Noriel one year later in March 1902, nor even with Malvar (who made him a guerrilla general) in April of that year.

It was in the same year, according to "official history," that war was supposed to come to its end. And Amado Guerrero sums up the colonial brainwash of Filipinos from that time on in four words: "Patriots were called bandits."

Katagalugan's Katipunero

MONTALAN THE OUTLAW remained in the hills with his guerrilla fighters. Together with Colonel Cornelio Felizardo, a fellow Caviteño from Bacoor, he carried on the struggle against the Americans—even if he had to do so this time against former comrades in the Revolution who were now on the enemy side, either as civil officials (like Trias) or as officers of the Constabulary or Scouts (like Bonzon).

It was Apolinario Mabini, the "brains" of the Republic, who said that if Aguinaldo fell, others would replace him—and that statement was made true by Malvar. When General San Miguel kept up with this tradition by taking over Malvar's own place in 1902, he certainly considered Montalan's Cavite holdouts a part of his army, as they had always been under Malvar. And when Ricarte in January of 1904 returned from exile to wage his own revolution (which flopped, incidentally, within two months), the "Vibora" readily had General Montalan in mind as his Division General for Southern Luzon. If Montalan did not accept this offer from his former commanding officer, it was because at that time he was already sworn to Macario Sakay's "*Republika ng Katagalugan.*"

To fully appreciate Montalan's role in history and see the significance of his metamorphosis from *Magdiwang revolucionario* to *Katagalugan* Katipunero, perhaps one must first understand *Katagalugan* which necessarily traces its roots to the Katipunan, but to which, unfortunately, historians of the past never even gave one short glance. It must be recalled that the secret society of plebeians originated in Tondo, where it was founded in 1892 by Andres Bonifacio and a few friends. Sakay joined it in 1894, when he was still in his early 20s, in the same year Emilio Jacinto was initiated. Being all "taga-Tondo," Bonifacio, Jacinto, and Sakay belonged to Tondo's *Katagalugan* Council which was, theoretically, the *Kataastaasang Sanggunian* from which all the other *sanggunians* of the Katipunan had evolved, including *Magdiwang* of Noveleta and *Magdalo* of Kawit. Those three Tondo boys formed the great triumvirate of "genuine Katipuneros" (*tunay na Katipunan,* to use their own term) who would truly work for the independence goal of the Sons of the People even to a point of fanaticism—all of them giving their lives, in fact, for that cause. When Bonifacio fell victim to *ilustrado* politics in Cavite in 1897, young Jacinto carried on the *Supremo*'s unfinished work. And when Jacinto himself died in 1899, outside the fold of Aguinaldo's *republica*, his rightful heir as *Supremo* of the Katipunan was no other than Macario Sakay.

In 1900, the Katipunan as a secret society was revived by Aguinaldo's republican forces in support of their guerrilla resistance against the Americans. Until that time, the Katipunan veterans organized by Bonifacio and Jacinto had been allowed to play mere bit parts (mostly as *sandatahanes,* or bolomen) in the drama of the Malolos Republic. And only then did those survivors of Bonifacio and Jacinto find an opportunity to reassemble and rearm themselves free of republican repression. This time, the Sons of the People were out not only to drive away the foreign aggressors but to rectify the manner of the struggle and redirect it to the "true path to Kalayaan" from which the exponents of the *republica* had strayed.

54

John R.M. Taylor's compilation of "insurrecto papers" shows that as early as January 1901, in the midst of the Aguinaldo-led struggle, Sakay, using his old Katipunan name "Dapitan," began calling on the brethren to come together again.

In subsequent documents, we know that this Katipunan revival by true Katipuneros was carried out in the name of *Katagalugan*, that is, the group originally founded by the Katipunan cadres of Tondo. Distinction must be made of this revival from that one launched in the name of the Republic by the men of *Magdalo* and *Magdiwang* who were responsible for its liquidation—as well as that of its *Supremo*—in 1897. In recounting the 1897 factional wars between *Magdalo* and *Magdiwang* adherents in Cavite, our own historians had completely overlooked *Katagalugan*. Yet, it was there all along in the persons of Bonifacio and his Manila group; and it was the third party in that intramural fight among rebels against which, being the proverbial outsider, the Cavite "republicano" factions would conspire as one in order to eliminate in the end.

And in 1901, though Bonifacio and Jacinto were gone, *Katagalugan* was still there to regain the *Supremo's* fallen crown in Tejeros, this time in the persons of Sakay and his Katipunan veterans. In August of that year, even as Malvar was taking over from the fallen Aguinaldo, *Katagalugan* was conspiring with non-republican *Magdiwang* diehards like the Alvarezes and the Villanuevas (they never fought under Aguinaldo) and with leaders of the budding *obrero* movement in Manila in an assembly held in Quiapo that gave birth to the *Partido Nacionalista*. Then, in December, the *Katagalugan* leaders, on their own, drafted a constitution to achieve legitimacy for their new revolutionary government repudiating Aguinaldo's republic—and, in effect, disregarding Malvar's assumed leadership.

But all this came to a halt in January 1902 with the premature arrest of Sakay and some of his associates in the *Partido* and in his own *Katagalugan* movement. Although Sakay would be included in the general amnesty of July 1902, he came out of prison to find his *Katagalugan* without leaders (they were either hiding or in jail). He also found the Partido Nacionalista taken over by another group—a new alliance of Manila *obreros* organized by the *ilustrado* agitators Isabelo de los Reyes and Dominador Gomez, and the peasant guerrilla bands in Rizal led by Julian Santos, Faustino

Guillermo, Apolonio Samson and others. These men, too, had been Katipuneros of the '96 revolution and had been friends of Bonifacio (Samson, for one, accompanied the *Supremo* to Cavite); but they were not "*taga*-Tondo," they were not of *Katagalugan*. And these men had elected, during Sakay's absence in jail and after Malvar's surrender, General Luciano San Miguel as the new generalissimo of the resistance forces.

If Malvar had been the continuer of the Republic and Sakay was the renewer of the Katipunan, San Miguel was now the synthesizer of both struggles who called for all factions and groups (he was a former *Magdiwang* who fought under the Republic) to unite and fight as one for national independence. Within a year, however, the nationalist San Miguel was killed in a battle which colonial historians chose not to remember, and his commanders fell one after the other to be incarcerated or hanged—as "bandoleros."

This was in March 1903. In May, Sakay reappeared on Mount San Cristobal in Laguna, starting all over again in the very region where Emilio Jacinto met his own lonely end. Sakay had personally taken to the field as *Presidente-Supremo* of the new K.K.K. government, which now stood for "Kataastaasang Kapulungan ng Katagalugan."

And Sakay had designated Julian Montalan—in Vic Hurley's English—"Captain General of the Armies of Liberation."

Bandolerismo's Generalissimo

THE ANNUAL REPORT of the U.S. Philippine Commission for 1903 reveals how Cavite holdouts Julian Montalan and Cornelio Felizardo "have from time to time given trouble," even extending their operations to Laguna where they raided towns like Cabuyao and Bay during the last quarter of 1902. But the Constabulary, after crushing the San Miguelista guerrillas in Rizal and Bulacan, next went after the "ladrones" of Cavite. The Montalanistas, however, managed to escape from the Constabulary dragnets, with Montalan himself finding refuge in the mountains around Tagaytay on the Cavite-Laguna-Batangas border with the remnants of his own band.

Meanwhile, Sakay was nearby at Mount San Cristobal in Laguna. It was there that he issued his first war manifesto in the name of *Katagalugan* in May 1903. And it was then that Sakay the plebeian-Katipunero and Montalan the peasant-*republicano* forged a new brotherhood in that sacred mountain haven of the Colorums, perhaps going through the Katipunan blood pact again, the "brothers" swearing to come to each other's aid and not to abandon the struggle for the *kalayaan ng bayang tinubuan* under the red banner of their "Republika ng Katagalugan." To symbolize this pledge, Sakay and Montalan vowed never to have their hair cropped until Inang Bayan was finally redeemed from the American invaders.

General Montalan's headquarters was at this time on Mount Gonzale, somewhere between Talisay and Bayuyungan (the present-day town of Laurel). The entire Tagaytay mountain ridge not only offered Montalan's guerrillas good hiding places and production bases (for planting root crops and vegetables), but also served as a strategic base from which Montalan could direct operations for the scattered *Katagalugan* forces ("outlaw bands" in Constabulary records)—those of General Aniceto Oruga in Batangas and Laguna, those of General Cornelio Felizardo in Cavite from Bacoor to Silang and Dasmariñas, and those of his own band from San Francisco de Malabon to Maragundon and Indang—of which he was now Generalissimo.

In case the enemy attacked his mountain camp, Montalan could easily find another and hide. He could also simply go east to Laguna and join forces with Major Gregorio Flores near San Pablo, or south to Batangas with Lieutenant-Colonel Fructuoso Bito near Taal or Colonel Andres Villanueva near Bauan, or north to Cavite with Colonel Masigla near Indang, Colonel Caro near Dasmariñas, and Major Giron near Silang. And when occasion called for a mass assault, all these guerrilla bands could easily converge upon a chosen target—as they did in the second raid on Bay (Laguna) in April 1904 and, later in January 1905, in Taal (Batangas) and San Francisco de Malabon (Cavite).

Colonel David J. Baker later commanded the combined U.S. Army, Cavalry, Scouts, and Constabulary troops who would pursue, kill and destroy these "outlaw bands" of *Katagalugan* under the overall personal command of Julian Montalan. In an official report of the Philippine Commission later in 1905, Baker made these rather unpleasant remarks on the *Katagalugan* fighters and their commanders:

Most of the leaders took part in the insurrection, and a few of them, including Julian Montalon [that spelling again!] . . . have never surrendered nor taken the oath of allegiance [to the United States]. All of them assume titles, and the organization and interrelations of the bands [they commanded] are theoretically military. However, the members wear no uniforms, and when pressed hide their guns and mingle with the general population. While they do not hesitate to maim and kill peasants and laborers who incur their enmity [for being pro-Americans?], they content themselves with maltreatment or abduction of more prominent natives, and rarely molest foreigners. The bands are usually recruited from the ne'er-do-wells of town and country, from misguided youths, and ignorant dupes.

Yet, this army of "ne'er-do-wells," "misguided youths," and "ignorant dupes" was *the* people's army—and certainly *not* the mercenary masses who had enlisted in the American army as scouts and in the colonial force as *constabularios,* nor much less the *principales* in the towns who had banded themselves into "civilian volunteers" who assisted the "lawmen" in many a posse hunt after those "badmen." Few as their numbers were, these guerrillas counted, however, with the full support of the greater barrio population who fed them, clothed them, and hid them from the clutches of the Americans and their allies. Especially in Cavite, the people were, as a rule, "in sympathy with the outlaws and warn them of the approach of the constabulary or scouts," as admitted by Constabulary Chief Henry T. Allen himself. In 1903, the civil authorities found it necessary to suspend all the town officials of San Francisco de Malabon—apparently for the reason that it was Montalan's hometown.

Proof of Montalan's wide acceptance by the people is the fact that even outside his native Cavite, his leadership was readily recognized by leading anti-Americans. In Batangas, for example, where "a good deal of the deviltry and about all the fight was taken out of them," in the words of General Allen in his 1903 report on post-Malvar insurgency to the U.S. Philippine Commission, the senior inspector of the Batangas Constabulary (Captain Ben Smith) submitted to Allen a blacklist of at least "ten who had taken the oath of allegiance, but have since joined the fraternity of cutthroats under Montalon [sic] in Cavite."

Included among those ten wanted men were Aniceto Oruga of Lipa, Fructuoso Bito of Taal and Andres Villanueva of Bauan—all ex-Malvaristas who swore allegiance to *Katagalugan,* not to America, and who acknowledged the authority of Sakay as

58

Presidente-Supremo and of Montalan as Generalissimo.

In August 1903, Sakay would be forced out of Laguna and, crossing Lake Bay on boats, he transferred the seat of his *Katagalugan* government to the Tanay mountains in Rizal. But Montalan himself remained for some time at his Tagaytay highland headquarters. There, as "Terror of the Mountain," to borrow from the poetry of Erwin Castillo, the Montalan legend surged further to towering heights.

Gorio Porto's "Treasures"

AMONG THE *GUERRILLEROS* who fought under Montalan was Gregorio Porto, a captain of his band, who lived until the 1960s. Captain Porto was among the guerrilla commanders tried for "bandolerismo" after the general surrender of the *Katagalugan* forces in 1906. He and Montalan escaped the gallows but were thrown into the old Bilibid prisons and, later, exiled to the Iwahig Penal Colony in Palawan. Porto was pardoned after serving ten years in Iwahig. He then returned home to Cavite—and to farming. In 1960, still a farmer, Porto was the only surviving member of Montalan's army and the only one left, he claimed, to reveal the secret of Montalan's "buried treasures in Cavite."

His, indeed, is the one and only published personal account on Montalan by a veteran of the latter's peasant army, as told to his nephew, Vivencio Porto, who explained that his uncle Gorio felt it was "his responsibility to let the readers know the truth, at least, before he died." Before the old man died, he left us this interesting account in the old *Manila Times*:

> I am no bandit, although my name has been linked with Julian Montalan, Macario Sakay, Lucio de Vega and others who sacked so many towns in Cavite, Batangas, Laguna, Rizal and Bulacan. . . .
>   Montalan and his 300 followers, including myself, lived in so many hideouts in Cavite and Batangas with Macario Sakay as *Supremo*. I was given the rank of Capitan with 115 men. . . . Although Sakay was recognized as our *Supremo*, he was not often seen with us. Our commander was Julian Montalan, the general who lived like Ali Baba in caves with treasures and 300 looters. . . . When the late Julian Montalan started as an outlaw in 1901, he did not realize he was setting a precedent for five or six decades of crime sensation [i.e., in Cavite, referring to such later-day legends like Tiagong Akyat in the 1920s and Nardong Putik in the 1950s]. Because of his kidnapping and treasure hoarding, he now lives in Philippine history [i.e., in "official history"] as one of the most

notorious outlaws, although in fact he was a kind and considerate man who had firm convictions.

As one of the late Montalan's closest friends, I know that the great outlaw's place in Philippine lore began to be etched one day when the President of the first Philippine Republic was captured by the Americans [with their Macabebe mercenaries] in Palanan in 1901.

Montalan took to the hills. For a living he and his armed band had to beg from rich Cavite residents. When the suppliers refused to help them any longer, Montalan's men [many of whom, like Gorio Porto himself, were probably farmers anyway] planted root crops near their hideouts. When they realized that the root crops they were harvesting were not enough, they started sacking towns and army camps for ammunition and food supplies at night, while staying in caves during daytime.

They lived in Mount Gonzale somewhere in Batangas. From there they organized 50 men and went to Cabuyao, Laguna to solicit the help of friends. While on their way they met a company of American soldiers with supply-laden horses. The Americans pursued them from Cabuyao to Tagaytay. In Tagaytay they were able to stop the advance of the American soldiers by burning the tall grass.

The enraged American soldiers spread posters announcing rewards for the capture of Montalan. Someone pointed his hideout in Mount Gonzale, so they had to hide in Mount Batulao. Because of the intensive search for them in several provinces, they had to stay in Mount Batulao for two years. To survive they planted corn, cassava and other crops along the slope of the mountain. They were clearing the slope . . . one day when Juan Moya, their guide, came to inform them that the location of their hideout was given to the Americans by one of their own officers.

Montalan unsheathed his sharp knife and in one stroke cut the lips of the officer. Juan Moya comforted Montalan by saying he could find a new hideout for them. Moya was known as the best guide in the troop. He knew the secrets of almost every mountain in Southern Luzon. From Juan Moya, they learned about Pinaglintikan cave in sitio Maytubig near Caloocan, Batangas. Their hideout in Maytubig was the best cave they ever had. They were staying in that cave when I joined them. . . .

"Among the officers who stayed in that cave known as Pinaglintikan," Captain Gregorio Porto recalled, "I am sure I am the only survivor. I am the only one left to reveal the secret of the cave, thus I feel it is my responsibility to let the readers know the truth."

Porto says he was taken to that cave by Montalan himself after an encounter with American troops in San Francisco de Malabon "sometime in 1901." (Was this a mental lapse, or was it a typographical error? Should the year be 1903?) Porto had suffered a bullet wound in the ankle during that fight, Porto claims, and Montalan took him along in his retreat to the Tagaytay ridge, treating his wounds with herbs and even assigning a junior officer of the band, Filomeno Peroy, as Porto's nurse. Porto and Peroy stayed in that cave for six months, while Montalan and his raiders went about with their "bandolerismo."

Here is Gregorio Porto's story on the supposed "treasures" of Julian Montalan:

After a raid, Montalan, Peroy and I used to talk about women and so many other things, but Montalan's buried treasures seldom got [into] our conversations.

One recalls that Montalan hid pieces of gold, silver pesos and pesetas in different places. Some people say that for every jar of buried treasure, Montalan had to kill a man with the mission that the ghost had to guard the treasure. Nothing as horrible was related to us by the late Montalan. . . .

Since the death of Montalan, reports about his treasures have stirred the imagination of treasure hunters in Cavite, Laguna, Batangas, Rizal and Bulacan. Someone said that a part of the treasure is in the hands of one of the most prominent figures of Cavite, a former disbursing officer of the late Montalan. Others say it is in a cave near Maytubig in Batangas, on the slope of Mount Gonzale in Batangas, [at] a creek in sitio Mandaluyong, General Trias, Cavite.

Barrio residents say that a farmer who found a part of Montalan's treasures in General Trias now owns a Cadillac and several apartments in Manila. And recently a grader operator bulldozed another part of the hidden treasures in Buenavista while the road from Dasmariñas to Trece Martires City was under construction.

While the roads connecting Naic, Trece Martires, Dasmariñas and Tagaytay City are under construction, old friends of Montalan believe that more treasures of Montalan would be unearthed.

Porto asks his readers: How did Montalan gather these treasures? And he answers his own query: "By kidnapping, looting houses of rich men, by volunteering as trustee of millionaires and raiding the same treasures he was supposed to guard." Porto further strengthens his treasure tale by recalling an incident in which he himself, he claims, was an eyewitness. He continues:

In 1904 [1905?], the younger brother of Julian Montalan, Bartolome, surrendered. Bartolome told the Americans that his brother, Julian, was hiding an enormous amount of money in the cave where I was staying with Peroy. Three or four days before the Americans arrived . . . a big monkey tried to scare me out. I killed the monkey and stretched the body on a bamboo pole, then rolled it in my old mat. In four days the dead monkey, stretched four feet, exuded the most horrible smell.

It was almost sunset when I saw Bartolome Montalan with a group of [Constabulary? Scouts? U.S.Army?] soldiers under a certain Lt. Kier [or was it Kerr?] hauling out the treasure of Julian Montalan. Beneath the waterfall they

61

found jewelry, silver pesos and gold trinkets, with Lt. Kier claiming all of it. They left the cave with handkerchiefs covering their noses. They could not stand the horrible smell of the dead monkey.

"Gorio's body stinks like hell," Lt. Kier told his men. Lt. Kier announced in my hometown that his troops found me dead at the cave's entrance. Thus, my sister, Eusebia, was surprised when I appeared two years later in the sala of Judge [Ignacio] Villamor.

Gregorio Porto adds that in his present (1960) occupation as a farmer, he had no more time to look for his friend's remaining treasures. He also says that Montalan later "died a rich man" in Iwahig—not because of his treasures, but because he had married there a rich Chinese trader's daughter. Porto remembers a Montalan promise his friend was not able to fulfill: "Siahong Gorio, Ate Ebyang, as soon as I could go back to General Trias [town], we are going to spend all my treasures within three days by giving the wildest party our hometown would ever witness." This statement of Montalan added weight to Porto's belief "that Julian Montalan's treasures are still hidden somewhere." But not even Porto knew definitely where those treasures lay buried.

And we who today read Porto's account in 1960, when he was no doubt already in his 80s, we wonder if his "Buried Treasures Lie Untouched in Cavite," written through a nephew, was not after all just another yarn—just one more Caviteño legend from those simple folks who helped the creative writer Erwin Castillo imagine his six-toed, asthmatic but ever romantic Montalan who "near the end, German agents had gifted . . . with a *baul* full of coins in payment for some secret, unheroic act."

Porto's story is here retold for the record and for its worth, before the account itself gets lost in a mountain of dusty periodicals. That being done, let us now dig into the very records of the Constabulary and read between the lines of those "official" reports which make up the bulk, unfortunately, of our sources on Montalan's daring guerrilla raids.

Montalan's Guerrilleros

THE MOST ACTIVE among Montalan's guerrilla raiders was the mysterious General Cornelio Felizardo—"slippery as an eel, dangerous as a black panther," as Vic Hurley described him.

62

Felizardo was comparatively a newcomer who had joined the "insurrecto army" against the Americans and who, like Montalan, had served under Generals Trias, Ricarte, Noriel, and San Miguel. He and Montalan had refused to join the general surrender with Malvar in 1902, and both of them were never amnestied. Felizardo remained intransigent even after the death of General San Miguel, and there was little hope that he would ever come down and swear to American rule. When he signed up with Sakay's organization in 1903, he virtually signed his death warrant, so to speak. From that time on, the Constabulary would declare a fight to the death against Cornelio Felizardo.

As early as 1903, Colonel William Scott of the Constabulary called him "the most troublesome outlaw in Cavite." He was at the time roaming about Bacoor and Imus with an armed band of only 40 men, among them his own brother Diego Felizardo. The U.S. Army and the Constabulary had been hunting down his guerrillas for two years—"without any success," Scott reported, because "his followers were such adepts in the rapid change from outlaw to *bien amigo*." Felizardo himself, on many occasions, was said to have been entering the towns to attend fiestas and cockfights.

The late Antonio K. Abad, in his book on Sakay, narrates a popular anecdote which fairly illustrates the personality of Cornelio Felizardo, undoubtedly the most curious character among Montalan's raiders. Being allegedly a *compadre* of ex-General Trias, now governor of Cavite, he once attended a party in the Trias house. "On occasions like this," says Abad, "Felizardo was very careful; before partaking of the food served to him, he first gave his dog a piece of meat to ascertain if the food was [not] poisoned." On that particular occasion his dog died, and the enraged Felizardo "turned the table upside down and began to shoot at everybody in sight." Finally he fled to the nearby hills, carrying away a woman named Justa who was said to be "an accomplice of the assassins."

But the Felizardo tale that has been told and retold especially among the poor folks of Cavite, and was accepted even by many *constabularios* themselves, was when he collected the 5,000-peso reward for his head by having his "dead body" delivered to the Constabulary. Peasants who knew Felizardo were called in to identify the body and they swore it was the man. Colonel D.J. Baker himself "was convinced that Felizardo was dead," writes Vic

Hurley—although Hurley adds that "the body of the man turned in for the reward was believed by many to have been killed by Felizardo himself." Later, in early 1906, a second reward was paid to two Constabulary men who had infiltrated Felizardo's band and did the killing themselves. But that's too far ahead of the story. Before Felizardo was finally killed, he would first make a reputation for himself as a fearsome—perhaps the most fearsome—guerrilla raider in Cavite.

One of Felizardo's commanders was Segundo Poblete. On the night of 12 November 1904, Poblete was sent by Felizardo to punish the "americanistas" in the Laguna border town of San Pedro Tunasan. But Poblete's men were not able to capture the municipal police station and the quarters of the scouts, their targets, and they soon retreated after their leader fell mortally wounded. Major Poblete later died from the effects of his wounds.

The San Pedro raid was probably a dry run. "In December 1904," Vic Hurley notes, "matters had become intolerable within a few miles of Manila." Hurley meant Felizardo's raid on Parañaque—the boldest yet in the history of the *Katagalugan* movement—early in December of that year. His spies had told him on 8 December that most of the *constabularios* in the Parañaque garrison would be out attending a fiesta in another town. Felizardo did not waste time. Cleverly, he disguised 75 of his best riflemen in Constabulary tunics they had captured in their past raids and, led by Captain Mariano Mendoza, ordered them to march into town. Once in town, the guerrillas quietly surrounded and then seized the cuartel of the Constabulary, killing a corporal, wounding two *constabularios*, and disarming all the rest. General Felizardo's guerrillas brought back 15 Springfield carbines, four revolvers and a lot of ammunition from their Parañaque raid.

An indication that the Cavite forces directly under Montalan were about this time ordered to go to Batangas could be gathered from a series of subsequent actions that culminated in the raid on Taal. That early part of December, a detachment of Constabulary under Lieutenant Grayson clashed with Colonel Masigla's force in Alfonso, killing one of its commanders, Major Alvarez. But Masigla soon joined up with Colonel de Vega from San Francisco de Malabon and together in a night ambuscade on 16 December, they almost annihilated another Constabulary unit at a place called Marquina near the Cavite-Batangas border. Then, crossing over to

Batangas with their men, they joined forces with those of Colonel Bito and attacked the garrison of Taal on 5 January 1905. On this occasion, the municipal officials secretly assisted the raiders, who succeeded in subduing the entire Constabulary and police forces of Taal. The guerrillas captured 20 rifles and 15 shotguns and also carried away 15,000 pesos from the municipal treasury of that town.

Fructuoso Bito belonged, of course, to Oruga's command. Not to be outdone, on 12 January, General Oruga on his own attacked the Scouts stationed in the town of Talisay on the other side of Lake Taal. This time the guerrillas were repulsed with a number of losses, among them one of Oruga's commanders.

A few words about Aniceto Oruga. One colonial account described him as "a villainous-looking thick-set man with a rapacity for young girls." But in Ricarte's memoirs, just as Montalan stands out in the ranks of *Magdiwang*, Oruga, too, occupies a prominent place as one of General Malvar's more intrepid officers. In the "first war" he distinguished himself, together with local hero Colonel Rosendo Banaag and that famous heroine "Henerala Agueda" in the four-day Battle of San Pablo (Laguna) during the second week of October 1897. When enemy reinforcements arrived from Lipa and Tanauan, these were ambushed by Oruga's rebel force who pursued the retreating Cazadores up to the outskirts of San Pablo, inflicting many losses on them and capturing all their rifles. And on another occasion shortly before the truce at Biyak-na-Bato, the then Colonel Oruga employed tactics using his own wife as decoy to lure a Spanish gunboat ashore—"seizing all its cannons and rifles, and killing with bolos all the Spaniards aboard except two" (according to Ricarte). Oruga, like Montalan, would recur as a fighter in the wars of '98 and '99 because of his association with the '96 rebel generals who went on to fight under the Republic. Oruga would surrender with them and swear allegiance to America, only to fight again later under Sakay and Montalan.

After the Taal and Talisay raids, all the guerrilla leaders— Felizardo, Oruga, de Vega, Bito, Masigla and Caro—consolidated under the overall command of General Julian Montalan for the grand attack on Montalan's native town of San Francisco de Malabon on 25 January. Of Montalan's personal command alone, more than 300 guerrillas took part in this raid. Again, they came in with a lead party of marching men in Scout and Constabulary uniforms. Again, it was a successful trick that made it easy for the raiders to seize the usual main target, the Constabulary *cuartel*, which yielded only 25 carbines and over 1,000 rounds of ammunition. They also took 2,000 pesos from the municipal treasury.

Elsewhere in the town plaza, other raiding groups fired on the officers' quarters and other buildings where the rest of the garrison had taken cover. A detachment of Scouts which was not a part of the garrison, being in Malabon on another mission, joined the fight. Their medical officer, Dr. O'Neill, was among those later killed by the fire of the raiders. The siege was long enough for guerrillas who were natives of that town to take time to visit their long-missed relatives. One group, Felizardo's, tried to capture the provincial governor, Don Mariano Trias, who had been Montalan's and Felizardo's commanding general under the Republic but whom they had now blacklisted as a collaborator (even if he was said to be Felizardo's own *compadre*). Trias managed to run away. The raiders then proceeded to loot his house, and then took away his wife and children.

Felizardo's abduction of his alleged *comadre*, Mrs. Trias, was perhaps done to score the poisoning attempt on Felizardo during the Trias party narrated by Abad. Montalan himself and Colonel Cosme Caro, second-in-command of Felizardo's guerrillas, when they learned of the incident, hurried off to Felizardo's mountain camp to intercede in behalf of the hostages. And accordingly, the Triases were set free. It was a gesture of kindness typical of Julian Montalan, an aspect of his character that would, sometime later, help save this folk hero from the gallows.

Hearing of these raids by Montalan and his peasant guerrilla bands, American oldtimers in the Philippines who were old enough to remember their Civil War days must have recalled William Clarke Quantrill's own "post-war raids" in Missouri. And, to some extent, there's quite a parallel. Many Americans today regard Quantrill's atrocious raids (legendary "badmen" Frank James and Cole Younger rode with his band, just as Felizardo and Oruga fought under Montalan) not as banditry, which was then the charge against his raiders, but as legitimate guerrilla operations. And the killings committed by them were, as time went by, understood as "necessary killings." Montalan the Insurrecto and Quantrill the Confederate were both "rebs." They were not *soldiers* fighting a gentleman's war, but mere *outlaws* who had smashed government military posts, looted the government treasuries, and murdered government officials and sympathizers. And the necessary cost or consequence of waging an underdog guerrilla war such as those waged by Quantrill and Montalan had always been ruthless retaliation.

What the American authorities did in Ilocos Norte in 1900 against Aglipay's guerrillas, in Samar in 1901 against Lukban's guerrillas, in Batangas in 1902 against Malvar's guerrillas, and in Albay in 1903 against Ola's guerrillas—they did not hesitate to do again, perhaps with less mercy, against the *Katagalugan* "bandits" of Cavite, Batangas, Laguna, and Rizal in 1905.

Inang Bayan's Montalan

LUKE E. WRIGHT had succeeded Governor Taft in February 1904. In his inaugural address on 1 February, Wright cast rhetorical aspersions on the Resistance while endorsing collaboration: "Every Filipino should turn a deaf ear to the sinister promptings of restless and selfish agitators and demagogues who strive to keep alive prejudices born of evil passions engendered by war . . . true patriotism under existing conditions is found in a loyal attitude to the [U.S.] Government."

One year later, by virtue of the "Cooper Act" of 6 February 1905, he would be the first American chief executive in the Philippines to be called Governor-General. And his initial act under this title was to declare martial law in the four Tagalog provinces most affected by the guerrilla operations of the *Katagalugan* forces: Cavite, Batangas, Laguna, and Rizal. Governor-General Wright suspended the writ of *habeas corpus* and authorized the "reconcentration" of the barrio population in those provinces. Wright's mailed fist policy transformed the four provinces of *Timog Katagalugan* into a single "special provisional district" placed under complete Constabulary control, thus reducing that southern Tagalog region into one vast concentration camp.

This was the Constabulary's first big test. And it was a contest where the *constabularios* could not afford to be outnumbered by a force that had outfought and outmaneuvered them numerous times. To make sure the operation would be successful, units of the U.S. Cavalry and the Philippine Scouts were ordered to augment the main task force of 1,200 crack Constabulary troops. And placed in command of all the forces was that hell-roaring U.S. Army officer of the Jack Smith-James Bell school(*) of vicious rebel-fighting—Colonel David J. Baker.

Reconcentration was more widely known—and feared—as the *zona*. As a repressive measure against insurgency, it worked out in 1902 against Malvar and again in 1903 against Ola in Albay. But in 1905 this policy was "without effect" in Cavite, according to David Barrows. This American writer admits that "Mr. Wright was ill-advised" on the matter of concentrating the inhabitants of the barrios. The method only brought about "a grievous hardship to many thousands of innocent people," but it failed to bring down Sakay or Montalan or Felizardo to submission.

"Crops were lost," writes Barrows, "property was destroyed, and a feeling of ominous bitterness was aroused." But Barrows did not say that the people were bitterest not because of the "bandits" of *Katagalugan*, but because of Colonel Baker and his "pacification" troops. The *ilustrado* General Jose Alejandrino, in his memoirs, remembers Baker as "sadly infamous for the cruelties he committed on persons accused of complicity with Sakay." Even Barrows concedes that the measures resorted to by Baker and his men were "lawless and indefensible and were neither properly investigated nor punished."

The people who suffered most from the *zona* were, naturally, Montalan's and Felizardo's townmates from San Francisco de Malabon and Bacoor. In Malabon, according to the Watson papers, the *reconcentrados* were taken from "all the barrios of the municipality." One line alone was formed by "1,500 men of all ages," including ex-Governor Trias himself (he was replaced by Colonel D.C. Shanks) and the previously suspended town officials, and out of this line 14 guerrillas were identified by former comrades who had been previously captured (and softened with the "water cure"?) by the Constabulary. In Bacoor, the principal suspect as "insurgent abettor" was the ex-general Mariano Noriel, who was said to be a cousin of Felizardo. The barrio of Ligas in Bacoor was a special *zona* target because it was there where Felizardo's family lived.

_____

(*)General J. Franklin Bell considerably reduced the male population of Batangas in 1902 to secure the surrender of Malvar. General Jacob Smith gave the order to "Kill anyone over ten!" in Samar to avenge the "massacre" of a full American company by Lukban's guerrillas in the town of Balangiga.

Martial law failed to break the back of *Katagalugan*'s mass following, whose decreases were accountable to actual deaths and not to defections. Just the same, the joint Constabulary-Scouts-Army field operations left a crippling effect on the resistance movement itself. In 27 recorded encounters, according to the Watson papers, the government forces recovered more than 500 firearms (including 61 carbines) and decimated the guerrilla ranks with "149 killed, 373 captured and 444 tried and sentenced to prison."

By June 1905, the Constabulary chief could report to the Philippine Commission the death, among others, of Colonels Caro, Masigla, and Villanueva; and the capture or surrender of General Oruga, Colonel Ramos, Lieutenant-Colonel Bito, and Majors Flores and Giron. With Felizardo's own killing by two government infiltrators in his band only months away, this left Montalan with but two remaining field commanders—Colonel Lucio de Vega in Cavite and Major Benito Natividad (not Aguinaldo's general from Nueva Ecija) in the Batangas-Laguna area—by the close of that year. And with its Cavite-Laguna-Batangas forces in such a sad state of decimation, Sakay's *Katagalugan*, though still alive in Rizal and Bulacan, faced a grim end.

The American chief of operations himself, Colonel Baker, thus gave this conclusion on that 1905 campaign south of Manila:

Felizardo, disarmed and stripped of companions, lurks between here [Bacoor, Baker's headquarters] and Manila. De Vega and his remaining followers skulk in the forests of Buenavista and Jalang. Montalon [sic] who has been joined by Natividad's remnant of Oruga's band is hidden now here and now there by the Colorum Society.

Felizardo was treacherously killed in March 1906. Whether patriot or scoundrel, he had lost his life as a fighter of *Katagalugan*, a true *Anak ng Bayan* who remained a holdout for *Kalayaan*. Following his death, Montalan, de Vega, Natividad, Porto, and their remaining diehards joined the general surrender of the *Katagalugan* forces in July. Montalan and his officers accompanied *Supremo* Sakay when he came to Manila on 6 July 1906 to formalize their surrender which, they were made to understand, was being pursued by the civil authorities—and by *politicos*—in exchange for the creation of the proposed National Assembly.

During this supposed period of negotiation, the *Katagalugan* leaders, perhaps naively, accepted an invitation from the new military governor of Cavite, Colonel Louis Van Schaick, to attend a *baile* in their honor. As it is now generally known, Sakay's officers were in the middle of a dance (except Sakay and Montalan who "really disliked mingling with the Americans," according to an account by General Leon Villafuerte of Bulacan) when they were surrounded and "captured" by the Cavite Constabulary.

Under the provisions of the Bandolerismo Act, General Sakay, General Montalan, General Villafuerte and Colonel de Vega were sentenced to the gallows; while General Carreon, Major Natividad, Captain Porto and others were meted out long prison terms. The charges against them were "crimes" committed by their forces in furtherance of the guerrilla law—better known as the Montalan Law—punishing every treasonable act by *americanistas,* as follows:

> For taking office under the American government—death.
> For giving information to Americans—cutting off the lips.
> For guiding American troops—cutting tendons of the feet.
> For giving supplies to Americans—crushing the fingers with rocks.

Montalan bravely accepted his fate and had someone write to his wife, Juana Laoren, on 11 September 1907: "Do not grieve for my coming death and absence from your side, for it is my fate and the will of God." And to his sister Victoria, on the same day he said: "The 13th of September is the day set for my disappearance from this world, that is, my execution, in compliance with the sentence imposed upon me by the will of God. . . . My last request is that I want you to look after my children and not to abandon them."

But on Friday the 13th of September that they were to have gone to the scaffold, clemency was extended to Villafuerte and Montalan. In the latter's case, his "criminal" records state the reason for his last-hour salvation:

With reference to Julian Montalon [sic] it may be said with truth that he was the least bloodthirsty and cruel of all the bandit chieftains who cursed the provinces of Batangas and Cavite. Confirmed criminal as he was, some of the milk of human kindness yet lingered with him, and when Mrs. Trias and her little babies had been carried into the mountains by a monster dead to every human sentiment [the reference is to Felizardo] he strove by every means of his power to save her from indignation and to accomplish her release. That she was released was due to his efforts and those of [Colonel] Cosme Caro, whose mother was induced by him to intervene on behalf of her unfortunate countrywoman. This act of mercy on the part of Julian Montalon shall count for something on his hour of extremity and weigh the balance in his favor when nothing else could save him.

But some would say Montalan was given clemency because influential fellow Caviteños and former comrades of his in the republican army, notably Tomas Mascardo and Emilio Aguinaldo himself (and General Trias, too?), personally pleaded for his life. And many still would swear none else but Montalan's *anting-anting* saved him from dying with Sakay and de Vega at the gallows.

Montalan's death penalty was commuted to life imprisonment in the old Bilibid prisons. Two years later, together with Gregorio Porto, he was exiled to the Iwahig Penal Colony in Palawan to continue serving his life term at hard labor. Porto was pardoned (in 1919?) after serving ten years in Iwahig, and Montalan's own pardon came two years later. Back in Cavite, the faithful Porto communicated fairly well with his friend and former chief through letters (Did Montalan still dictate his letters and sign his name with an "X"?). Thus, he learned how Montalan, after regaining his freedom, captivated the heart of a rich Chinese trader's daughter in Iwahig. If the famous Montalan *anting-anting* on women was still good, so was his talisman for wealth: the Montalan couple engaged in farming, cattle-raising, and the trading business—and all these enterprises prospered in a few years.

Meanwhile, back in Cavite, Juana Laoren herself lived in with an American army officer who, Porto claims, "seemed to be more interested in the treasure of Julian Montalan than in the former Mrs. Montalan." After a few years, that Yanqui soldier of fortune did find part of the treasure, according to Porto, and he hurried off to America without even saying *adios* to Juana Laoren. Poor Juana died penniless, survived by her two Montalan offsprings who were cared for by Montalan's sister, Victoria. Son Victor, as Porto writes his account in 1960, became a farmer in Amadeo (Cavite), and daughter Matea went to live with her father in Iwahig.

Montalan died "a rich man," in Porto's words, before the Japanese Occupation. But to the Montalanistas—the peasant guerrillas who fought under him, like Gorio Porto, and in general the Cavite peasantry who had fed and sheltered his anti-imperialist

71

fighters, and whom he loved in return—he was their hero until the end.

If, indeed, Julian Montalan was an outlaw, nevertheless he was a great one. He was one of *Inang Bayan*'s greatest holdouts against U.S. imperialism in his time, and he was outlawed by the Americans and their *americanistas* because of his revolutionary stand. Had *Katagalugan* won its independence war, no doubt Montalan would have been among those remembered and honored on National Heroes Day. And the town of San Francisco de Malabon, his hometown, would not now be named after the *ilustrado* son who accepted compromise with the American rulers, but after the peasant hero—the Julian Makabayan—who remained true to the original independence goal of the Revolution.

3

GLORY AT
THE GALLOWS

**RETRACING THE HARD ROAD
OF MACARIO LEON SAKAY
FROM CRADLE TO SCAFFOLD**

three:

GLORY AT THE GALLOWS

The Plebeian as Patriot

"*ADIOS FILIPINAS!*" These were the last words of General Macario Sakay at the gallows, according to the *Manila Times* reporter on the beat at the old Bilibid Prisons that morning of 13 September 1907 when the Americans executed the "self-asserted President of the Philippine Republic."

It was a Black Friday. And that made it all the more symbolic, because that Friday the 13th of September in 1907 marked the final agony and death of the Katipunan in the person of its last surviving apostle. Sakay's Filipinas could have been personified by one lonely figure in the crowd that stood waiting outside the prison walls: "a woman seen [by the reporter] weeping, as a scraggly-haired dog pawed sympathetically at her dress."

General Sakay and his associate Colonel Lucio de Vega were hanged for banditry—"bandolerismo"—and the hanging had angered many Filipinos. Before the two revolutionary officers died, Manila residents demonstrated in front of the Malacañan Palace to protest their execution. But the American Governor-General refused them an audience with him. Frustrated at Malacañan, these same people made one last attempt at the Bilibid to wrap the remains of Sakay and De Vega with Katipunan flags. But, again, the demonstrators were thwarted by the prison authorities.

Nationalist patriot? Revolutionary guerrilla? Folk hero? Maybe he was all that—and a martyr besides—but Macario Sakay is certainly the most maligned resistance leader in the history of Philippine libertarian movements.

"Sakay occupies a position that fringes on the fantastic and the

75

heroic," the historian Teodoro Agoncillo, introducing Abad's book, once opined. "He was a twentieth-century Don Quixote who fought blindly, perhaps naively, against what he thought were the evil forces that dissipated the trembling hopes of those who, nurtured in the Malay tradition of glorious self-sacrifice, learned to accept defeat with blunt misgivings."

Agoncillo's statement was made in the mid-1950s, when thus far the only ardent biographers of Sakay were Jose P. Santos and Antonio K. Abad, respected non-scholars whose lack of profundity in their works was compensated, however, by their wide use of first-hand documentary evidences in presenting their hero's case to a long-misled public. In the next decades the verdict on Sakay came favorably with the upsurge of nationalist-viewed interpretations of history, as taught by Agoncillo.

"He spelled Resistance," Maria Elena Abesamis wrote for the old *Sunday Times Magazine* in 1969, ". . . a Resistance lengthy and arduous enough to convince the enemy that the Filipinos meant to keep and rule over their own."

By the 1970s, nationalists who were scholars and historians were more explicit in their judgment. "A people's hero . . . a brave patriot," said Renato Constantino in 1975. "A victim of jaundiced history . . . a glorious diehard, incredibly brave and tenacious, a stubborn straggler and hold-out for independence," wrote Carmen Guerrero-Nakpil in 1976.

And in 1981, Sakay's latest biographer, Rod E. Cabrera, said of his Hero: "His life may not be as well-documented as Rizal's or Bonifacio's but its quintessence had all the makings of heroism equal to, if not surpassing the heroism, if at all, of those whom we continue to venerate."

It was a long, hard road for Macario Sakay from cradle to scaffold. But it was an even longer, more difficult way back to his rightful place in our history after the American victors wrote their own version and blotted out his name in those days of nationalist suppression in the early 1900s, of which he was both a symbol and prime mover. After the last generals of the Republic fell, Sakay symbolized and led a movement that was both protest to collaboration and resistance to America's "benevolent assimilation." This was the reason why that particular stage of our struggle for national independence had been belittled, damned and deleted in propaganda passed off as history by the Americans and their

Filipino lackeys. There had been reluctance to accept Sakay even as a minor historical figure because the American- imposed legend pictured him completely as a villain.

Agoncillo again: "Thanks to the early Americans and their sympathizers, Sakay lived on, even after his execution, as a long-haired bandit—a Robin Hood without his virtues."

The Americans likened our Sakay to their Quantrill: an ornery postwar guerrilla leader dedicated to nothing more than loot and pillage. This bad-guy image is typical in an early American-made "Philippine History" textbook in which the author, David Barrows, lines up the heroes of the 1903-1907 revolutionary struggle—Sakay, Montalan, Felizardo and de Vega—as "perhaps the most desperate and most cruel leaders in the history of the insurrection."

Vic Hurley, who wrote an account of the Philippine Constabulary under the Americans, calls them the "Unsavory Quartet." And he singles out Sakay as the "organizing genius" of what all American writers of the period coined as "ladronism"—from the Spanish *ladron,* meaning bandit.

But isn't this treatment of Sakay's movement as simple *ladronismo,* what was really unsavory and cruel? It is a cruel misrepresentation, if not a wanton distortion of History!

Macario Leon Sakay was a plebeian. Like his friends Andres Bonifacio and Emilio Jacinto, he was from Tondo, that traditional cradle of rebels from the days of Soliman and Magat Salamat. According to the late Antonio K. Abad in his work on the hero, Sakay was born in 1870 of obscure parentage and out of wedlock. The surname is said to be his mother's. If Sakay was luckless enough to end up an outlaw and at the gallows, it's simply because the poor fellow got entangled in various complications which seems to be the common fate of our plebeian heroes of the Revolution.

Bonifacio, Jacinto, and Sakay form the great triad who personified in succession the Katipunan and the revolutionary masses: "the sons of the people." They were true-blooded proletarians, sons of Tondo, representative have-not *indios bravos.* Because of their revolutionary convictions, they led heroic and tragic lives. By founding the Katipunan, Andres Bonifacio sparked the Revolution that would only reject and eliminate him. By propagating the *Supremo's* work, Emilio Jacinto was ignored and left alone to die by the Republic. Did Macario Sakay meet a similar fate, too, for inheriting the leadership of the Katipunan?

Pro-American quarters regarded Sakay as no better than a mere cutthroat. To them he was a highway robber under the guise of taking over the anti-American resistance from the fallen generals of the Republic. Their main argument was that he did not belong to the Revolution, that he was not under the legitimate framework of the Republic, and that he was therefore just a self-styled patriot who hadn't fought and lost—"with respectability"—the war against the Americans.

But they forgot that Sakay was of the Katipunan. Sakay was an original Katipunero—"*tunay na Katipunan*," in the language of his comrades. Where else had the Revolution taken roots from before it stemmed into Aguinaldo's Republic? It had sprung from the revolt of the masses sowed by the seeds of the revolutionary Katipunan! Why then despise the surviving Katipunan veterans who made a comeback in the 1900s for rearming and continuing an armed struggle they had started in the first place? Why then classify them as lesser patriots—nay, outlaws—simply because they adhered to the idealism of Tondo and not to the conformism of Kawit or Malolos which rejected (or feared?) them?

Sakay may not have belonged to the Revolution we are familiar with (1896-1902) which was, after all, a mere transition in leadership from the masses to the middle-class. But he was one of the main protagonists of the whole revolutionary period (1892- 1907) which started with the Katipunan and ended with it. As someone in the nationalist newspaper *Pagkakaisa* had written in an inspired moment, Sakay was "a burning ember left from the first fire of the revolution to keep the cauldron of struggle simmering on." Sakay, in this case, was the Last Katipunero.

But the last warrior of the Katipunan was also among its first recruits in Tondo, having joined the secret proletarian society in 1894, the same year Emilio Jacinto did. The 24-year-old Sakay rose to become president of the popular council "Dapitan," which was an offspring of an older council in Trozo, the "Balangay Silanganan" headed by his friend (and future right-hand man) Francisco Carreon. Sakay was therefore one of the hardcores of the *Katagalugan* Council of Tondo, or what Bonifacio was fond of calling "Haring Bayang Katagalugan," that sired all the other *sanggunians* of the Katipunan. Gregoria de Jesus, Bonifacio's widow who later became Mrs. Julio Nakpil, recalled how Sakay helped the young Emilio Jacinto put out and circulate the *Kalayaan* and other papers of the Association. "Macario Sakay was a true patriot," she later wrote in her autobiography; "I know he greatly helped the Katipunan."

It is strange that we should know more of the Katipunan during its *secret* stage than when it finally came into the open to lead the Revolution. After the outbreak in 1896, our materials get scarce even on Bonifacio and Jacinto themselves. Of Sakay, we know he took part in the early battles against the Spanish forces. Agoncillo in his *Revolt of the Masses* says Sakay was there with Bonifacio, Jacinto, Faustino Guillermo, Apolonio Samson, Francisco de los Santos and Hermogenes Bautista in the Montalban hills where, having vowed to fight to the end, they mapped out their next battle plans, beginning with an attack on the town of San Mateo. Certainly he was there when the actual battle of San Mateo was fought, first in the town proper where the Katipuneros were victorious, then along the Nangka River where they lost heavily this time. Happily, Sakay survived, and he was probably again by the side of his Tondo friends in the retreat to Balara.

But it seems he was not with the group that accompanied the hapless Bonifacio to his doom in Cavite. Only Francisco Carreon, Apolonio Samson, and Alejandro Santiago—we learn from Artemio Ricarte's memoirs—were among the top Katipuneros of Manila who are said to have crossed over to Cavite with the *Supremo*. And these names are especially mentioned here because they would recur in the attempts of Bonifacio's orphaned Manila Katipunan to rise on its own—outside of Aguinaldo's *republica*— in the 1900s.

It would be wrong to think of every Katipunero of Manila (and that includes Morong, later named Rizal) as truly loyal followers and believers of Bonifacio, or as true apostles of the Katipunan's "sacred ideals." That may have been true only of the original cadres from *Katagalugan*, such *taga*-Tondo as Jacinto, the Carreons, and Sakay himself. Of Bonifacio's later recruits outside of Tondo, only those from Balara, perhaps, would fight by his side until the end—their leader, Lucino de la Cruz, indeed losing his life in that struggle and dying a *Bonifacista*. But Pio del Pilar of Makati, Ramon Bernardo of Pandacan, and Vicente Leyba of San Juan (whom we know better as "Heneral Kalentong," his *nom-de-guerre* in the

Katipunan)—they and others would switch loyalties once already in Cavite. And even the likes of Apolonio Samson, Julian Santos, Faustino Guillermo, and Luis Malinis were never really "ideological" Katipuneros who lived by and died by the teachings of the society. They were peasants from outside the city who, by themselves, formed a separate wing of Manila Katipuneros who were often in discord with the policies of the supreme *Katagalugan* council of Tondo. Santiago Alvarez in his memoirs, *Ang Katipunan at ang Paghihimagsik*, tells how at Balara on the eve of Bonifacio's departure for Cavite, Luis Malinis confronted the *Supremo* on the issue of money. And yet, when "Heneral Luis" fell gallantly at the battle of Novaliches not long after, who can deny that he had fought and died as a true "*anak ng bayan*" *for* the "*bayang tinubuan*"?

Sakay may have remained in Balara with Julio Nakpil. Or he may have gone to Laguna with Emilio Jacinto, who never ceased "katipunizing" that region until he died, never joining the generals of the Republic in their struggle against the Americans. In the iconographic archives of the Ayala Museum there is a rare photograph of the dead Emilio Jacinto as he lay in state, his mother and wife by his side. Two unidentified Katipuneros in the background, even without the moustache and the long hair, look familiar—are they Macario Sakay and Francisco Carreon?

At any rate, Sakay's name is never mentioned in any popular account of the Philippine-American War. But his activities around this time may have been purely organizational and totally underground in furtherance of Bonifacio's—and now Jacinto's—unfinished work in the Katipunan. This is, at least, the reading one gets from an account of Pio del Pilar. This "brother" in the Katipunan (he was initiated into the "Magtagumpay" council of Culi-Culi by Bonifacio himself) who went over to Aguinaldo's side and became a general of the republican army, had never doubted Sakay's patriotism. In a letter to Jose P. Santos in 1930, Pio del Pilar said:

Macario Sakay, as I knew him, was a true *makabayan*. In the days of the revolution [Aguinaldo's revolution?] while we [in the Republic?] were doing the fighting, he on his part was spreading the Cause of the Katipunan whose ultimate objective was to win the independence of the Philippines. He was among those who greatly helped by going from town to town [in 1899, 1900, 1901?] to organize the councils of the Katipunan. This passion for that Cause was so great that even when the Americans caught him [in 1902?] he was still determined to consummate the unfinished Katipunan goal to make the

80

Philippines free and independent, by means of promoting a new revolution.

Sakay may have been a bandit in the eyes of the Americans. That's why they sent him to the gallows. But before God, Country and Truth, he was a true *makabayan* who deserves to live in the minds of all countrymen for all times.

The Abad (or was it Gregorio Zaide's?) translation of Pio del Pilar's original version in Tagalog missed the whole point of this letter and so also missed the very essence of Sakay's patriotic labors in behalf of the Katipunan—which could have easily answered Abad's questioning subtitle for his book on Sakay: "Was he a bandit or a patriot?". And this was because Abad failed, in the first place, to make a distinction between Del Pilar as a *republicano* soldier and Sakay as a purely *katipunero* organizer. Del Pilar wrote his account in answer to questions on his alleged involvement with Sakay in 1904, as evidenced in some documents of the period. Granting without admitting that he got involved, Pio del Pilar suggests in the letter that Sakay's was a true patriot's cause which, though its path may have differed from the one del Pilar chose to follow (the Republic's), nevertheless sought the same goal of Philippine independence.

General Pio del Pilar, when captured in 1900, refused to swear allegiance to America. He would later join fellow "irreconcilables"—like Mabini and Ricarte—who were deported to Guam in 1901 for their intransigence. After his return in 1903, contemporary documents would implicate him as one of Sakay's generals.

Had the Katipuneros-turned-Republicanos turned Katipuneros again in the 1900s?

The Patriot as Katipunero

KATAGALUGAN WAS THE KEY to Macario Sakay's rightful place in History, but the History lost to Oblivion. One accepts Sakay as Katipunero—as *tunay na Katipunero*—only if one simply puts *Katagalugan* back to its own obliterated historical role.

Katagalugan was the Katipunan of Tondo. As such it was the parent council, the very first Katipunan cell that would, eventually, be outgrown and outclassed by its very offsprings in Cavite: the Katipunan of Noveleta (*Magdiwang*) and the Katipunan of Kawit (*Magdalo*). In the end, our own historians would only remember *Magdalo* and *Magdiwang*, forgetting the parent that was never for once even mentioned in any history book, nor was it ever taught in any history class. Because *Katagalugan* was snubbed by History (or was it by her *ilustrado* historians?), so were all those Tondo revolutionaries who remained *tunay na katipunan* even after Bonifacio's and Jacinto's deaths—Sakay, Carreon, Nicdao, Santiago, and all the others—for whom *Katagalugan* meant both the native town (Tondo) and the native land (Filipinas). And so today in Tondo, not one *callejon* and not a single *eskinita* commemorates any *Katagalugan* fighter's name—with the sole exception, perhaps, of Moriones (though, for sure, people who have gone to the Tondo plaza bearing his name never knew who he was and what he did).

And yet, Tondo remembers (and honors with streets) the elite "katipuneros" of a much, much older brotherhood: Magat Salamat, for example, or Pitonggatan, or Manuguit. These men, together with such other *maguinoos* as Juan Banal, Martin Panga, Taumbakal, Calao, and Maghicon, led Tondo's first "Katipunan" that challenged the second generation of white aggressors in old *Katagalugan*—"the land of Tagalogs"—in the tradition of Rajah Soliman's resistance which ended with his death in 1571 at the Battle of Bangkusay. But before they could raise their own "cry," Tondo's first "katipuneros" in 1587 (as in 1896 and 1906) were betrayed, rounded up, and either incarcerated or exiled or hanged. Three centuries later, as if group karma wanted to prove its truth, their spirits lived again in an Andres Bonifacio, an Emilio Jacinto, a Macario Sakay, a Francisco Carreon, a Domingo Moriones, an Alejandro Santiago—but this time as a *plebeian* conspiracy. Tondo in the 1890s may have lost that glory and grandeur it once enjoyed as the center of old *Katagalugan* in the 1580s, but not its revolutionary Malay tradition. The Katipunan of Bonifacio and Jacinto may have lacked the *cacique* standing of Salamat, Manuguit, Pitonggatan, et al., but not their *maguinoo* and *indio* attributes. *Ilustrado* histories remembered those Tondo warriors of the 1580s and paid lip service, at least, to their 1896 "incarnates," but totally erased from respectable memory the last holdouts for *Katagalugan* in the 1900s.

Tondo in the 1900s was the hub of the city underground, as it was in the early 1890s when the Katipunan was founded, after the bourgeois-led *Liga Filipina* disintegrated with Rizal's exile to Dapitan. Manila's dreaded "Arma Blanca," that phantom army of bolomen whom General Luna had so much depended upon in his bold attack of Manila at the start of the war with the Americans, enlisted its recruits mostly from that place—from the hotbeds of Trozo, Palomar, and Binondo. There, a guerrilla base awaited the "Conquering Regiment of the Viper" during Ricarte's own planned revolt in the city mid-year of 1900, before he was caught and deported to Guam. And there, too, even as the *republica* sustained its *ilustrado*-led struggle against the Americans, the old workers of the Katipunan rose again.

Late in 1900 the dramatist Aurelio Tolentino, himself an original Katipunero, one of the few who had gone to college (at Santo Tomas), recruited from among his fellow Katipunan veterans in Tondo a group of urban guerrillas called "Junta de Amigos." Between *zarzuela* scenes, which Tolentino would write and direct, his actors played real-life partisan roles and made life miserable for the Americans and their collaborators in Manila. The many mysterious fires and *dukot* assassinations that took place in the city during 1900-1901 were definitely pinpointed to this group. The disappearance of the Creole captain of the Manila secret police, Lara, nemesis of such *revolucionarios* as Artemio Ricarte and Pio del Pilar, may have been the work of the Junta.

Sakay's role in the Junta is not discernible. But it is almost certain that two documents of this period, which John R.M. Taylor included as exhibits in his compilation of "insurgent records," were drafted by Sakay and his own *Katagalugan* group. In one document (which Taylor presents as Exhibit 1140) a certain "M.S. Dapitan" signs as "Lieutenant-General" in transmitting "orders received from the General Headquarters of the Army" to the "Honorable Brigadier-General of the South" who, in turn, countersigns as "Bulalakaw." This circular dwells on seven points which, Dapitan says, he makes known to all "for the sake of good order and the better organization of this venerable Katipunan." Here is a summary:

(1) Katipunan members are entitled to religious freedom.
(2) Members guilty of treason and insubordination will be punished "without clemency."
(3) Civil officials who conceal such crimes will likewise be punished.

(4) *Dukot* will be practised in punishing all traitors.

(5) Any such punitive act must be reported to headquarters through echelons.

(6) Any member of the society who brings in 100 rifles becomes a captain in the "regular army."

(7) Any nonmember who joins the society and presents 100 rifles will likewise be rewarded.

The first document is dated 6 January 1901 in Manila. The other document (Taylor's Exhibit 1144) is dated 8 February 1901 and appears as *Order No. 2*. "With a view of improving and perfecting the organization of the Katipunan ng mga Anak ng Bayan," the document begins, "on this date this second order is published . . . and the other previously promulgated [the 6 January document?] is hereby repealed." Then *Order No. 2* proceeds with a lengthy discussion on the functions of "town commissioners" and the local committees composed of a president, a secretary, a judge and a treasurer—an organization no different from the Katipunan popular councils in the 1890s. Seals appear on the margins, notes Taylor, which read as follows: "K.K.K.—EXECUTIVE COMMITTEE" (Was it "KATAASTAASANG KAPULUNGAN" in the original?) and "Military Headquarters, Supreme Commandery ("comandancia suprema"?) of the Katipunan of the Philippines." Again, this document was signed by "M.S. Dapitan, Lieutenant-General."

Who was "M.S. Dapitan"?

Aurelio Tolentino would have been an easy guess, if Francisco Carreon had not practically given away the answer in his own account given to Jose P. Santos in *Ang Tatlong Napabantog na "Tulisan" sa Pilipinas*. The Carreons, two brothers and a cousin, joined the Katipunan the very same year (1892) it was founded. Like all original Katipuneros who went through the secret rites and blood pacts, Francisco Carreon was known by a Katipunan symbol: "*Ang pamagat ko'y F.C. Silanganan,*" he reveals. "F.C." were his initials. And "Silanganan" was the Katipunan name for one of the popular councils of Trozo (similar to the "local committees" mentioned in Taylor's exhibits) of which he was its president. The other *balangay* was known as "Dapitan" and its head was, of course, Macario Sakay. So who else could be "M.S. Dapitan"?

And who was "Bulalakaw"?

Santiago Alvarez in his memoirs cites the *Bonifacista* Miguel Ramos as carrying that Katipunan *nom-de-guerre* in 1896. He led one of the bolo companies during Bonifacio's disastrous attack on San Juan del Monte in that battleground now memorialized as Pinaglabanan. This "Bulalakaw," says Alvarez, was among those captured in that battle and later deported to the Carolines, not to return until after the Americans came. But the Alvarez account on "Bulalakaw" ends there, and one can only surmise that Miguel Ramos "Bulalakaw," like most *Bonifacistas,* possibly soon rejoined his old circle of *tunay na katipunan* to resume work in the manner described by Pio del Pilar in his letter to Santos and in the documentary exhibits presented by Taylor. Could the "Bulalakaw" of 1896 be the same "Bulalakaw" of 1901?

But if our assumptions are all true, we only know at this point that Sakay was a "Lieutenant-General" receiving orders from the "General Headquarters of the Army." We can be certain it was not Aguinaldo's Republican Army. And surely it was neither Malvar's, since that would come later in April (not January or February) of 1901. And if there was a new Katipunan Army in 1901, who could have been its new *Supremo*?

Next to Bonifacio, the Katipunan could only be moved by Emilio Jacinto. After Jacinto, all the Katipuneros of Tondo—Sakay, Carreon, Santiago, del Rosario, Moriones, and others of the *Katagalugan* Council—were natural successors. But at a time of struggle still dominated by Aguinaldo's *republica,* not one of these men could certainly have stood up to the stature and prestige of *el presidente Magdalo*—unless that man had been Aguinaldo's co-equal, at least, from the old rival *Magdiwang* Council of Noveleta. And that would be Santiago Alvarez.

Was there a *Magdiwang-Katagalugan* plot to rearm right in the midst of the republican struggle?

All these conjectures are not at all far-fetched. For on 21 August 1901, the Partido Nacionalista was formed in Manila, in what may be called the "Quiapo Assembly"—having been convened in that district in a printing house on Calle Gunao. This came about only a few months after the Katipunan (i.e., the "true Katipunan" and not the Katipunan revived with the consent of Aguinaldo in support of his guerrilla war against the Americans) issued its first two decrees already cited.

85

But this time, the personalities involved in that gathering were identified by their names. Knowing the events that led to the Quiapo Assembly, the outcome of the election of officers during that founding session of the Partido Nacionalista should not be surprising to anyone:

Presidents	Santiago Alvarez
	Pascual Poblete
Vice-President	Andres Villanueva
Secretary-General	Macario Sakay
Counselors	Francisco Carreon*
	Alejandro Santiago*
	Domingo Moriones*
	Aguedo del Rosario*
	Cenon Nicdao*
	Nicolas Rivera*
	Salustiano Cruz*
	Aurelio Tolentino
	Pantaleon Torres
	Valentin Diaz
	Briccio Pantas
	Lope K. Santos
	Pio H. Santos
	Valentin Solis
	Jose Palma

---

*Katagalugan faction

One looks at these names and immediately notes the absence of any Aguinaldo follower in the group, dispelling comments by contemporary American writers that this Partido Nacionalista of 1901 would later dissolve because of discordant elements of the old Aguinaldo-Bonifacio rivalry. What is visible here is a gathering of *Bonifacistas*, and they may have been divided among themselves.

The old *Magdiwang* Council of the Katipunan in Cavite, the pro-Bonifacio wing, is represented here in the person of Santiago Alvarez, from whose memoirs of the Revolution we have already quoted a number of times. He was the son of Mariano Alvarez, a remnant of the Burgos era and onetime *capitan municipal*, who was the *Magdiwang*'s president. Santiago Alvarez himself was the Generalissimo of *Magdiwang*, as Emilio Aguinaldo had been of *Magdalo* (Kawit). The seat of *Magdiwang* had been Noveleta, which was known by the same Katipunan name. General Alvarez was known among the Katipunan brothers as "Apoy" and he would live up to that fiery war name: in the battle of Noveleta early in November 1896, his *Magdiwang* army would crush the better-armed Spanish troops sent to destroy his capital.

When the *Supremo* was caught, tried, and executed by the *Magdalo* forces on the charge of counterrevolution, Santiago Alvarez counseled against a civil war—brother againts brother—a bloody intent ignored by fellow *Magdiwangs* who were for unity, like Luciano San Miguel. But while many *Magdiwangs* including his own cousin Pascual Alvarez, and later San Miguel himself, would fight for *Magdalo* as the Republic, Santiago Alvarez was forever Bonifacio and forever *Magdiwang*. He would not go to Biyak-na-Bato or Hongkong, nor rejoin Aguinaldo after his return. Neither would he join the rebellious Jocson in the latter's attempt to usurp, in 1898, the leadership of the Katipunan. In all these actions he shared a conviction with Emilio Jacinto. But while we know a little, at least, of Jacinto's own work during the 1898-1899 period of the Revolution, information on Alvarez (his memoirs, unfortunately, ends with the downfall of *Magdiwang*) is zero—until he emerges again in the Quiapo Assembly.

It is possible that after Jacinto died in the middle of 1899, outside the fold of the *republica*, Santiago Alvarez came out of his isolation to carry on where Andres Bonifacio and Emilio Jacinto, his *compañeros* by choice, had failed. It is possible that he called upon the old faithfuls of the *Magdiwang* and *Katagalugan* councils (for they were, one must bear in mind, the only true *Bonifacistas*) to band together again to consummate the unfinished Katipunan goal through the correct path. And it is possible that this was the Katipunan Army that we see surfacing again in 1900-1901, with "Dapitan" (or Sakay) as Lieutenant-General and Alvarez himself (as "Apoy"?) acting as General-in-Chief, as he had once been in the army of *Magdiwang*.

If that was the case, then there were two wings of the new Katipunan, as there had been in 1896-1897, only this time they were factions among *Bonifacistas.* For Sakay's group, Alvarez must have been useful only to them as long as Aguinaldo was in the field. In a confrontation with the Republic, only Alvarez (who was an *ilustrado* himself belonging to Cavite's *principalia*) could stand up to Aguinaldo's level. But as the President of the Republic fell in 1901, so did the influence of Alvarez wane in the new Katipunan disguised as the Partido Nacionalista.

While Alvarez and Andres Villanueva, representing the *Magdiwang* group, were nominally on top of the Partido Nacionalista as president and vice-president, respectively, yet their roles must surely have been as mere figureheads. The real moving figures would be Macario Sakay himself—as secretary-general—and his *Katagalugan* group of Tondo Katipuneros whose names above are marked with asterisks. These men, in fact, were the very people who would, in a short time, displace the *Magdiwangs* and completely take over the leadership of the radical nationalist movement. This explains why all subsequent documents of the period would be drafted in the name of *Katagalugan*—which, henceforth, meant not only the old provincial council of Tondo but, as Andres Bonifacio had always equated it, the whole *bayang tinubuan.* Conscious or not, the Katipunan veterans of Tondo had, at the Quiapo Assembly of 1901, recouped the *Supremo's* fallen crown at the Tejeros Assembly of 1897.

There were, of course, other nationalist groups in the Partido aside from *Katagalugan* and *Magdiwang.* And these were linked to *Katagalugan*, either by association in the original Katipunan-Masonry circle of Bonifacio (Diaz, Tolentino, Torres, Briccio Pantas) or in the new *obrero* movement (Poblete, Palma, Solis, Lope K. Santos) that was from the start radical. One wonders why, at this time, there seemed to have been no direct link with the few armed bands of Katipunan veterans in Rizal (Guillermo, Samson, Santos) who were even then already active in the nearby hills.

The whole thing about the *Katagalugan* movement becomes clear when one notes that the Partido Nacionalista was created shortly after William Howard Taft assumed office as the first civil governor of the "Islands" on 4 July 1901. Was Sakay's group, until then underground, trying to "seek legal status"—as Reynaldo C. Ileto keenly observed in *Pasyon and Revolution*—through a lawful front like the Partido Nacionalista?

After the Quiapo Assembly in August 1901, it is easy to connect events in the chronology of Sakay's movement. On 2 November 1901, the "true members of the Katipunan," as they called themselves, drafted the constitution that would legitimize their cause. And the following month, on Christmas Day, they ratified that constitution and set up their new "Government of Katagalugan" under a *presidente-supremo*, a vice-president, and a minister each for War, Government, State, Justice, Hacienda, and Fomento. Of the 90 signers of that constitution, only ten comprised the main cell: Francisco Carreon, Alejandro Santiago, Cenon Nicdao, Domingo Moriones, Aguedo del Rosario, Nicolas Rivera, Salustiano Cruz, Patricio Belen, Feliciano Cruz, and Pedro Mendiola. And of these men, the first seven represented *Katagalugan* in the central committee of the Partido Nacionalista and, automatically, comprised the *junta suprema* of its own provisional revolutionary government. *Katagalugan* had been the Katipunan name by which Tondo was known among the "brothers," but it was now the name for the whole Philippine archipelago, for the whole Filipino nation. Bonifacio's "cry" in 1896, according to his followers, had been "*Mabuhay ang Katagalugan!*" (which was why other Manila Katipuneros outside of *Katagalugan* sometimes belittled it as *"ang unang sigaw ng mga taga-Tondo"*). And his official seal as *Supremo* of the Katipunan had proclaimed the *Kataastaasang Kapulungan ng Haring Bayang Katagalugan* as "builder of the Katipunan and initiator of the Revolution." *Katagalugan* was of course overshadowed by the *Magdalo-Magdiwang* merger which would, by 1897, essentially become the *republica*. But *Katagalugan*—from Bonifacio, to Jacinto, and finally to Sakay—never deviated from the path of the Katipunan.

Not the Republic's *Marcha Nacional Filipina* was its battle hymn, but the Katipunan's *Marangal na Dalit ng Katagalugan*. And not the three-colored, three-starred and eight-rayed sun emblem Aguinaldo brought from exile was its war flag, but Bonifacio's own red standard with the ancient Tagalog script "K" (for Katipunan? for Kalayaan? for *Katagalugan*?) in the middle of the "furious sun of *Katagalugan*": *ang poot ng araw ng Katagalugan*, to borrow the metaphor of Andres Bonifacio "Maypag-asa" himself.

The Katipunero as Guerrilla

THE HOUR HAD COME for Macario Sakay and Francisco Carreon. Now they came forward to occupy the two highest positions in the *Presidencia Suprema* of the new K.K.K. government: the *Kataastaasang Kapulungan ng Katagalugan*—Supreme Council of *Katagalugan*. Macario Sakay was the new Bonifacio and Francisco Carreon was his Jacinto. Alejandro Santiago was Minister of Government. Domingo Moriones was Minister of War. The Minister of State was Nicolas Rivera. And the rest of Sakay's "war cabinet" was filled up by the self-same personalities identified with him in the Partido Nacionalista.

"Sakay's Katipunan, with its emphasis on keeping alive the revolutionary style of Bonifacio's Katipunan, could not have been heir to the *ilustrado*-dominated revolution that preceded it," writes Reynaldo C. Ileto in his "new" history as he cracks open the problem of previous historians who saw the Katipunan and Republican struggles as one and the same revolution, as having one and the same goal. "To talk of a continuum in the struggle for independence, to assume that a common meaning of 'independence' existed for all," Ileto points out, "eventually leads to the conclusion that the post-1900 Katipunans were superfluous because they 'failed,' while the *ilustrados*, because they played the game of collaboration with the new rulers expertly, managed to attain more and more self-rule for the country."

The mistake most historians made in the past in ignoring *Katagalugan* and therefore failing to see it as the Tondo Katipunan resuscitated in the 1900s, also made it hard for them to under-stand—or much less defend—the charges of banditry on Sakay and his companions from both the Americans and the "genuine" *revolucionarios*. But again, Ileto clears up this matter:

> Who was genuine and who was false? The Americans and their local allies certainly tried to propagate the notion that the remaining insurgents [after 1902] were "false patriots," nothing more than bandits. The Katipunan, on the other hand, insisted that it was the bearer of authenticity. . . . To them, "Aguinaldo's revolution" had strayed from the path that the movement of 1896 had chosen. "Revolucionario" leaders, on their part, hardly recognized the post-1901 Katipunan as the legitimate continuation of their movement; joining in the American chorus of bandit accusations against Sakay and his group was simply another way of disclaiming continuity. Most of the "revolucionario" leaders acquiesced to and collaborated with the new colonial order as part of the game

of flexibility and expediency which the Filipino elite has been known to play exceedingly well. Unfortunately, it has been thought much too often that the rest of the society simply swayed and bent together with their elite patrons, and that those who did not were really outside society, i.e., bandits and religious fanatics.

The late National Artist Lamberto V. Avellana launched his filmmaking career by directing the monumental Filipino motion picture *Sakay* in 1939 but, in retrospect, must have rued his ambivalent, *ilustrado*-inspired character portrayal of the "bandit" —for, in fact, the heroic part went to the "Great Profile" Leopoldo Salcedo, while Avellana thought it ideal to cast that abominable "pre-war" *contravida* Salvador Zaragoza in the film's title role. And half a century after Avellana's Sakay, the *burgis* view of the "bandit" is reversed to the other romanticized extreme in Jose (the general's grandson) Alejandrino's 1982 historical novel *Insurrectos!*—but here, too, Alejandrino's "good-guy" Sakay, like Avellana's "bad-guy" Sakay, do not live up to historical reality. For instance, there's this scene where the novel's hero, Miguel de Cordoba (the mestizo ex-*insurrecto* captain who becomes, in the story, Sakay's defense lawyer) figures in a fictitious confrontation with his former chief, Emilio Aguinaldo, and the dialogue goes like this:

"You did well to defend Sakay," said Aguinaldo. "He was an *insurrecto* like us."

"Unfortunately, it changed nothing," said Miguel. "The Americans will hang him."

"Yes, the Americans will hang him. They need to set an example. But Sakay will remain a symbol. The people won't forget him. You see, Don Miguel, what's important are symbols and what they represent. In political conflicts, individuals are not important. They're mere historical accidents ... I became that symbol only by fluke of history. The people needed someone to rally to, someone to look up to, a symbol, and it happened that I was there at the time. A mere historical accident. True, we lost the war, but the symbol remains. It's like a torch that will continue to burn, a torch that will pass from generation to generation. After me, after you, there'll be other Aguinaldos, other Cordobas, who'll pass the torch. Look what happened. After Aguinaldo came Sakay. He was going to pass the torch and that's what made him dangerous to the Americans. That's why they need to make an example of him. But after Sakay, there'll be other Sakays until the Philippines finally is free."

It is a fine inspirational piece for a case for national unity and reconciliation (in this case, of *Aguinaldistas* and *Bonifacistas* making peace) but, unfortunately, distorts history. General

91

Alejandrino's grandson clearly espouses liberal or even progressive ideas, yet his "neo"-*ilustrado* mind ("educated mainly in Europe," says his resume) perceives only one and the same symbol—one and the same "torch"—of two extremely polarized figures. He does not see that Aguinaldo, by then, was the symbol of Surrender who could pass to no one a torch already extinguished in the first place, whereas Sakay was truly *the* symbol of Resistance whose burning torch of the Revolution, passed on from Bonifacio and Jacinto, would be picked up after his death by a long line of peasant armies and workers associations. There would be other Aguinaldos and other Cordobas, yes, but they themselves would be the extinguishers of the revolutionary torch and it was the other Sakays— and other Montalans and San Miguels and Ricartes—they united against (as in *Magdalo* and *Magdiwang* uniting against *Katagalugan* in 1897) to discourage them from passing *their* torch: the Light of the Katipunan in the armed struggle for Philippine independence.

Our previous failure to make distinction between the Katipunero and Republicano (or Revolucionario) struggles was the very reason why it took us all of seven decades to see Sakay's guerrilla movement as a legitimate Katipunan (and therefore patriot) endeavor outside that waged by Aguinaldo and carried on after his capture by Malvar. And if Malvar, after Aguinaldo's fall, issued his call to proclaim himself supreme commander of the "insurrection" in the name of the Republic, Sakay would do the same thing in the name of *Katagalugan*, the *tunay na Katipunan.* Certainly, neither one recognized the other's authority. If there was any link at all between these two nationalist movements, one led by *ilustrados* and the other led by plebeians, this was only a superficial one made possible by the existence of the Partido Nacionalista. And even such a link could not have lasted for long because of the Constabulary busts that would soon take place.

The Philippine Constabulary was created by the American civil government based on the racist dictum that "the best soldiers for dealing with the black man, the red man, the yellow man, and the brown man are the black man, the red man, the yellow man and the brown man"—words attributed to General George W. Davis, onetime commanding general of the U.S. Army in the Philippines. Vic Hurley, who wrote a history of the Constabulary under the Americans, said it in clearer terms:

> The Constabulary was a unique and successful application of the principle of employing native infantry, officered by white men, in the subjugation of their own tribesmen. Other nations had used the principle of native soldiers but the Constabulary developed a fundamental difference in the application of the force. This insular police unit fought the natives of a district with troops recruited in the same district.

And as a legal weapon to suppress the continuing anti-U.S. struggle of the 1900s, waged by both katipuneros and republicanos, the civil authorities passed the so-called Sedition Law, which defined *sedition* as any act of advocating independence by peaceful or any other means. Depicting Katipunan theater scenes (as Aurelio Tolentino's *zarzuelas* did) was sedition. Mouthing Katipunan slogans (as Pascual H. Poblete's *El Grito del Pueblo* did) was sedition. And displaying or keeping Katipunan flags (as the new Katipunans did) was sedition. By the bounds of this law, the Partido Nacionalista was a seditious organization teeming with Katipuneros—at a time when "the name Katipunan came to mean *terrorist*," as William Henry Scott phrased it in a recent work. As a consequence, its leaders were arrested by the Constabulary and were eventually silenced by threats of incarceration, if they were not already incarcerated.

The *Katagalugan* movement itself suffered an initial blow with the premature arrest of Sakay and Nicdao, among others, in January 1902. This led Alejandro Santiago, acting as *Presidente Supremo*, to resort to a policy of self-defense by reactivating the "bastard" (that is, unaligned) Katipunan armed bands in the hills of Rizal and Bulacan under the command of Julian Santos, Faustino Guillermo, Apolonio Samson, and other 1896 veterans—who were, however, though friends of Bonifacio or even *Bonifacistas* themselves, not sworn to *Katagalugan.* The Constabulary had suspected members of these bands to have participated in the strikes of the *obreros* organized that January by Isabelo de los Reyes, the famous propagandist who had returned from Europe with socialist ideas.

But all these only made things worse for the movement. After Malvar surrendered, the American authorities passed another legal weapon, the so-called Bandolerismo Act, which outlawed the existence of all armed bands and declared their formation by any group as punishable by death. Under General Henry T. Allen the Constabulary intensified its work by increasing its network of *secretas.* Through these spies, the ex-*insurrecto* General and now *constabulario* Lieutenant Licerio Geronimo caught the KKK supreme council in session in Marikina on 7 July 1902 (a strange coincidence, for it was on a same day in 1892 that the Katipunan was first founded). Acting *Presidente-Supremo* Alejandro Santiago was able to escape, but Aguedo del Rosario and Domingo Moriones were captured, and were later given long prison terms for the crime of sedition.

That previous 4th of July—what O.D. Corpuz considers "the mischievous Fourth of July of 1902"—U.S. President Theodore Roosevelt on the occasion of the anniversary of the Declaration of American Independence declared that all Philippine "insurrectos" be given "full and complete pardon and amnesty." But here's the mischief: the pardon and amnesty had excluded "persons committing crimes since 1 May 1902"—therefore excluding Moriones, del Rosario, or all the others. Sakay and Nicdao were luckier that time: being in prison since January and not having committed any crime "since 1 May 1902," they were included in the general amnesty.

There's a gap on Sakay's whereabouts from the day he was amnestied in 1902 to the time he appeared again on Mount San Cristobal (in Laguna) in 1903. One can only conjecture that he came out of prison to find his colleagues both in the Partido Nacionalista and his own *Katagalugan* group either in hiding or in jail. To replace the incarcerated Poblete, Dr. Dominador Gomez, another ex-propagandist in Europe who had come home, took over as president of the Partido. Gomez had communicated with the remnants of Malvar in Cavite, particularly with General San Miguel, himself an ex-*Magdiwang*, and with the peasant guerrilla bands in Rizal that Alejandro Santiago had activated in Sakay's absence. With Gomez coordinating the movement in the city, according to his own fashion, these bands had agreed to consolidate under General San Miguel's supreme command. One will note that Francisco Carreon who was never caught and who must have fled to the hills, too, was never linked to Julian Santos or Faustino Guillermo, or Apolonio Samson—all Katipuneros outside *Katagalugan* who would fight in San Miguel's army—although they and Carreon had all been "brothers" in the same revolutionary society founded by Bonifacio. Likewise, these "brothers," when Sakay surfaced again, would not unite in struggle with the

94

Katagalugan movement, in spite of the fact that a Sakay associate —Santiago, who acted as *presidente-supremo*—was the very one who had called them to arms. During that "gap" in Sakay's whereabouts, Santiago chose to remain with the San Miguelistas and was among those rounded up with them after San Miguel's untimely death in March 1903.

It is ironic that Sakay and Carreon as the last apostles of the Katipunan would, in the end, turn to the remnants of the Republic they would replace—the peasant holdouts in Cavite and Batangas led by Julian Montalan, Cornelio Felizardo, and Aniceto Oruga. And out of this peasant-plebeian alliance came forth what Reynaldo Ileto has properly termed the "Republic of Katagalugan" —not the misnomer and meaningless "Tagalog Republic" we read in earlier works (including even Constantino's) that totally obliterated the *Katagalugan* movement. Historians who wrote of this "Tagalog Republic" were misled by their own mistake and they therefore missed the whole point of Sakay's work in 1903-1907 as a continuation of Bonifacio's and Jacinto's—not Aguinaldo's—own work. It was not, as we would term it today, just any crumbly tactical alliance; *Republika ng Katagalugan* was a covenant as much as it was a brotherhood, the use of "Republic" being a concession to the republicano-provinciano peasants who provided the armed base, and *Katagalugan* being accepted by this peasant base of the overall (if nominal) Katipunero-Manileño leadership of the Tondo workmen.

This return of Sakay immediately followed General San Miguel's death at Corral-na-Bato during the first quarter of 1903. The survivors of the Constabulary dragnets "hid their guns and took shelter in Manila and the towns and barrios," the Constabulary reported later in the year. One San Miguelista group in Marikina, led by Tomas de Guzman, fled as far as Bataan where they were finally tracked down and rounded up in July. Julian Santos, then Benito Santa Ana, then Faustino Guillermo (with Alejandro Santiago), then Ciriaco Contreras fell one after the other. Only Apolonio Samson, the "terror" of Novaliches, was still at large by the end of 1903, but he was never heard from again.

In May 1903, according to Constabulary reports, "Macario Sakay took abode about Mount [San] Cristobal [in Laguna] . . . and recruited a few men." There, on 6 May 1903 (not 6 May 1902 as it appears in the works of Santos and Abad, because Sakay was still

95

in prison at the time), he issued his first war manifesto since his release from jail.

"It has been seen," Abad translates the first part of that manifesto, "that during the revolution in the Philippines, all our countrymen have no unity, and this lack of unity is caused by love of money, wealth and knowledge; courage is lacking to all, only self-interest is paramount." In its original Tagalog, Sakay must have sounded indeed much like his idol and mentor, the Bonifacio of 1896.

Sakay's manifesto went on to announce the creation of the "Kapulungang Katagalugan," to remind all "true Tagalogs"(*) not to turn traitors to the native land by not contributing aid and comfort to the American-sponsored government, and to warn the collaborators and mercenaries of the Americans. The residents of Manila, especially, were enjoined to "show their loyalty as true Tagalogs" by swearing allegiance to the "Katagalugan Government" and not to the American flag. Then the manifesto concluded by soliciting the loyalty and faith of the people, and exhorting them "toward the attainment of unity."

This manifesto of 6 May 1903 was Sakay's answer to the Sedition Law and the Bandolerismo Act. It was his call to the masses for a people's war, his challenge to American imperialism, and his warning to the erring countrymen—the *americanistas*—who had accepted the Yanqui rule.

And he signed this war manifesto with his own name as "Ang Presidente Supremo."

The Guerrilla as Outlaw

A NEW PEOPLE'S ARMY was born in the cradle of the Sierra Madre. And it was a guerrilla army whose leadership and core was neither *principalia* nor *ilustrado.* Not Malvar the landowning *indio,* not Trias the well-to-do *provinciano,* not Cailles the refined mestizo, not Macapagal Lacandola or Makabulos Soliman the *maguinoo*

(*)Andres Bonifacio and Emilio Jacinto themselves define this term in *Katipunan ng mga A.N.B—Sa May Nasang Makisanib sa Katipunang Ito:* "*Sa salitang tagalog katutura'y ang lahat nang tumubo sa Sangkapuluang ito; sa makatuwid, bisaya man, iloko man, kapangpangan man, etc., ay tagalog din.*"

descendants—not such men roused up this new Katipunan army risen from hibernation, but leaders molded from among its very plebeian ranks: Sakay the barber, Carreon the blacksmith, Montalan the unlettered, Oruga the unrefined, Felizardo the untamed—men collectively and derogatively classified in what Renato Constantino calls "official history" as *ladrones, tulisanes,* and *bandoleros.*

Cornelio Felizardo and Leon Villafuerte would be commissioned as division generals commanding the guerrilla zones south and north of Manila, respectively. Aniceto Oruga was among those appointed brigadier-generals, in command of Laguna-Batangas. Pio del Pilar, who had returned from exile late in 1902, would be carried in Sakay's roll of generals and may have accepted the commission, though he obviously never took to the field. Raised to the rank of "Captain-General of the Armies of Liberation"—as Hurley termed it—was that legendary hero of the 1896 revolution in Cavite: the illiterate but charismatic Julian Montalan.

Sakay was, of course, the overall leader as the *Presidente Supremo.* He would personally take command of Rizal province when the seat of his government was established in the Tanay mountains called *Di-Masalang.* The city of Manila itself, which maintained the city committee, was assigned to Francisco Carreon who held the positions of vice-president and executive secretary with the rank of Lieutenant-General. Sakay and Carreon were the only ones left of the *Katagalugan* leadership present and elected during the Quiapo Assembly of 1901.

Of the "ministers," all the previous appointees of 1901 having been imprisoned, only a comparatively unknown personality, one Fidel Noble, appeared in documents as "Acting Minister of War." But "Fidel Noble" has a curious ring: was it, perhaps, another nom-de-guerre? It is indeed a descriptive title most apt for those two faithful and noble Katipuneros of Tondo—Sakay and Carreon—truly the last two of the true sons of *Katagalugan.*

A few words on Francisco Carreon. The Carreon brothers of Tondo were among Bonifacio's first recruits of the Katipunan in 1892. The younger and more active of the brothers, Francisco, rose to the society's highest body, the Supreme Council, before the outbreak of the Revolution in 1896. Before that, he presided over "Balangay Silanganan," one of two popular councils of the Katipunan in Trozo, the other being "Balangay Dapitan" presided over by Macario Sakay.

97

Francisco Carreon was with the Katipunan leadership in all their important meetings, from Bitukang Manok to Pugadlawin to Montalban. Where the *Supremo* fought and lost, Carreon also bled: at Pugadlawin, at Balara, at Pinaglabanan, at San Mateo. Where the *Supremo* was mocked and vilified for his lowly origins, the faithful Katipunero was persecuted with him. He was there at Limbon when the *Magdalo* forces caught up with the *Supremo*'s diehards on their way back to Balara. But Carreon was luckier to escape the sad fate of the murdered Bonifacio brothers and his own elder brother, Nicomedes Carreon.

Santiago Alvarez includes Carreon among the *Bonifacistas* tried by court-martial with the *Supremo* in Cavite. The former *Magdiwang* chieftain also flayed Carreon and his fellow Manileños for not fighting it out to the death in defense of their *Supremo*. Carreon in his own account narrates only his escape: he was concerned about his family, whom he managed to bring out of Cavite to safety in Emilio Jacinto's camp in Laguna. There he helped young Jacinto in his work of spreading the Katipunan's revolutionary gospel, possibly with Sakay too, though Carreon didn't say so. Carreon went back to Manila in 1898 and was carried away by the *independencia* fever, organizing volunteers from Tondo to fight for the "second revolution." That experience under the Republic was brief and unpleasant, though, as his unit was disarmed and disbanded after they bungled an attack upon the Spanish forces in Santa Mesa, clashing by mistake with Aguinaldo's American "allies."

Like most of the Katipuneros from Tondo and Balara who went to fight in Cavite, he never wore any military rank, but the Aguinaldo forces knew Francisco Carreon was one of the *Supremo*'s generals. Like many Katipunan veterans he would rally to Aguinaldo's call in 1898, he would forget the intrigues of the past, he would again exhort the "sons of the country" to fight for the country. But, like all those of his class, Francisco Carreon was not allowed to play any role in the drama of the Malolos Republic.

Aside from Carreon, two other names date back to the infant days of the Revolution when the sole people's army was the Katipunan and the only *Supremo* was Andres Bonifacio: Julian Montalan and Aniceto Oruga. Montalan had been a minor figure of *Magdiwang* who became renowned, however, as a fearless and ferocious fighter. And if Montalan was an epitome of

98

machismo in Cavite—the classic *tirong* of Tagalog lore—so was Oruga in the Batangas-Laguna front where he became famous as one of the more intrepid officers under General Malvar. Both Montalan and Oruga occupy prominent places in the memoirs of General Artemio Ricarte, with whom they later fought as soldiers of the Republic.

Carreon, Montalan, Oruga, and all the others were, of course, the "bad guys" of those early American empire days, their guerrilla activities the "bandit phase" of the Philippine-American War, and their revolutionary government in the mountains the "organized band" of long-haired outlaws and fanatics. They really must have been rude, or roguish, or even mad. "It is believed," remarked Captain W.S. Grove about Sakay in 1903, "that this man is crazy." They were a far cry, indeed, from the fine crop of *ilustrado* gentlemen who led—but later abandoned—the good fight. But if outlaws they really were, no one can refute the fact that these "Robin Hoods and Jesse Jameses" (to quote James Blount) of Philippine history were the only patriots around to fight for *independencia* against American imperialism at a time when he who bowed to the Yanqui was *the* scoundrel.

Juan Cailles y Caupamme was, in contrast, a gentleman in the truest sense. An offspring of a Frenchman and a British-Indian woman, this half-breed did not have any *indio* blood running in his veins. But he was born and bred a Batangueño in Nasugbu. A product of the *Escuela Normal* run by the Jesuits in Manila, he was (like Ricarte) a schoolteacher in Cavite when the Revolution came.

His adventurous *burgueso* blood pushed Señor Cailles into the ranks of the *insurrectos*—first in the ranks of *Magdiwang*, then in the *Magdalo*. Aguinaldo was immediately charmed by this young, handsome, mustachioed French mestizo who did make a fine showing in the early battles. Ricarte, on the other hand, had little admiration for Cailles whom he holds responsible for the defeat of the *Magdiwang* forces in the Battle of Lian (3 October 1896)—"as the Spanish reinforcements from Balayan had succeeded in passing his men hiding in ambush and he had not notified headquarters." Later, the *Supremo* would order his arrest, because Señor Cailles had joined those who accepted the general amnesty offered by Spanish Governor-General Lachambre.

When the second revolution of 1898 came, he would fight again under Aguinaldo. When the war with the Americans broke out, he was second chief of the 2nd Zone of Manila, next in rank to General Noriel. When the guerrilla war began, he was general in command of Laguna, replacing the surrendered General Rizal. His guerrillas would score a few victories over the Americans; as a guerrilla leader, he himself would order a few killings, not unlike those charged later against Sakay and his companions. When Aguinaldo took the oath of allegiance to America, Cailles, too, swore to American rule. And even the *americanos* would find Señor Cailles so charming that they were willing to forget all about his "war crimes," appointing him instead as governor of Laguna. This was in 1901.

Now in 1903, Governor Cailles hears of an intruder disturbing the peace in his province, lurking in his mountains, proselytizing his people and, worst of all, usurping the title that had once belonged to his erstwhile "mi Presidente Emilio Aguinaldo." Señor Cailles certainly would not want to share the governorship of Laguna with any troublemaker, much less with an illiterate *bandolero* who was thought to be crazy. So he mobilized his municipal police forces and recruited a posse of volunteers from among the *principales* and ex-*revolucionarios* of his towns. And with the help of the Constabulary, Governor Cailles soon mapped out his battle plans to drive away Sakay and his "bandits" from Mount San Cristobal.

As early as 8 April 1903, Governor Cailles learned of Sakay's presence in the province when the *policia* of Nagcarlan captured nine of his guerrillas, obviously on a recruiting mission. The Sakay manifesto circulated in May. On 18 June, Juan Cailles personally led a combined force of Constabulary and police in an attempt to surround Sakay on San Cristobal. After a short fight, however, Sakay escaped to Mount Banahaw. But he was still in Cailles' territory and finally, in August, the enraged governor put up a stronger force and forced Sakay out of Laguna.

From Mount Banahaw, Sakay slipped into the Laguna lake area and from there crossed by boats to Rizal. From then on, Sakay set up camp and issued his circulars in the mountains he named *Di-Masalang*, between Boso-boso and Tanay. General Leon Villafuerte, who commanded the *Katagalugan* forces in Bulacan, describes the camp the first time he visited it, as Abad quotes and translates him:

On the seventh day of our travel [from Tanay] we met a group of picked men led by a certain Comandante Marcos. We learned the soldiers were sent by Sakay to escort us to his headquarters.

Now began a five-hour uphill trek. There were slopes on the way but we went up higher altitude at every ascend. At the first outpost we reached, the atmosphere was already misty and cold. We were stopped for identification and then ordered to move on.

We passed the third outpost at about high noon. The sun was a mere smudge and the weather damp, biting and dense. We found ourselves shivering with cold. Then we sighted a clearing naturally fortified with stone boulders all around it.

Passing through a small aperture in a huge rock and descending some two meters deep into a clearing, we finally arrived at a veritable army camp composed of about eighty huts, all roofed with rattan leaves. We were led to a bigger hut in the center of the barracks. There we were told to wait. I knew this was it—the General Headquarters.

The Constabulary and the Scouts were never able to locate and drive Sakay out from these headquarters. The *Presidente Supremo* may have been reported in some other place at various times, but the seat of his *Katagalugan* government and the general headquarters of his Katipunan army had always been in that mountain camp. By 1904, the *Katagalugan* forces in Rizal were growing to a considerable size that began to alarm the American Civil Governor himself. Early in the year Ricarte the Vibora had returned from Hongkong, and Sakay immediately sent his commissioners to confer with him in Tondo. "This government is waiting for your assistance," Sakay greeted Ricarte on stationery with his official seal as *Presidente-Supremo* of the Republic of Katagalugan. But Ricarte had plans of his own and would not subordinate these plans(*) to Sakay's existing organization. Once more two Bonifacio hero-worshippers—one a Katipunero, the other a *Republicano*—had failed to come to terms.

The Constabulary thought, at first, that Ricarte's presence would create a serious disturbance. But within two months, the Ricartista "revolution" was crushed. And the next expeditions would be directed mainly against Sakay, with the result that

---

(*)The Ricartista dream envisioned a different government—"provisional and dictatorial" in nature—directed by Ricarte himself but with *Junta de Amigos* leader Aurelio Tolentino (one of the stalwarts of the Partido Nacionalista) as nominal head.

"several times during the year this band has been located and a number of its members killed," according to Constabulary reports. In March, an expedition under Lieutenant Pitney struck a guerrilla camp 15 kilometers north of Tanay and killed 19 guerrillas, but failed to locate Sakay's headquarters, which was just nearby. Constabulary *secretas* were fielded to extract information or foment intrigues in the guerrilla camps. Five such spies tricked a number of Sakay's raiders into entering Boso-boso where the municipal police in hiding felled four of them. By way of retaliation, Sakay ordered a *dukot* for the *presidente* of Boso-boso.

Among the documents used as exhibits against Sakay during his trial in 1906 was a military order supposedly issued to Pio del Pilar as "Division General" instructing him on 17 May 1904 to enter the town of Teresa to "arrest the *concejal* Maximo Gravillas and all persons concerned with him in detaining our commissioners and as soon as arrested you will punish them as provided in Order No. 9 of 10 April 1904, prescribing that the tendon achilles shall be cut [for guiding American troops?] and the fingers of both hands crushed [for giving supplies to the enemy?]." Del Pilar was also reminded that "should the town people offer resistance to the [guerilla] troops, burn all the houses, without showing mercy to the inhabitants." Contemporary constabulary records, however, never named Pio del Pilar in any of Sakay's operations nor confirmed any raid on the town of Teresa led by him.

It was also in the month of May that the condemned San Miguel associate, Faustino Guillermo, was publicly hanged in Pasig. For the Constabulary, Julian Santos at the gallows would have been more symbolic, for it was he who had carried out that bold (and, for the *constabularios*, embarrassing) Christmas eve raid on Pasig in 1902. But Santos, though tried and sentenced to death, had earlier "cheated the gallows by dying in prison"—as the Constabulary worded it. So General Faustino Guillermo must now hang in Pasig. If Sakay knew it beforehand, he made no effort to prevent the hanging, or at least create a disturbance in protest of the execution.

At this time, too, another San Miguelista, Colonel Ciriaco Contreras, who had escaped the dragnet in 1903, was traced to a barrio in Cavite where he had hidden himself for more than a year disguised as a fisherman. Colonel Apolonio Samson, who escaped in Bulacan, was about the only San Miguel follower unaccounted for by the Constabulary by 1904. And he had not joined (nor was he asked to join) Sakay's movement, whose man in Bulacan was the young Leon Villafuerte. Hard pressed in Rizal that summer of 1904, Sakay in June tried to contact Villafuerte in Bulacan. But before they could even reach Norzagaray, the *constabularios* foiled that strategic move and forced Sakay's guerrillas into a fight where a few of them were captured or killed.

Was there a wishful thinker in 1904 who ever thought how far the Katipunan could have gone with General San Miguel and General Sakay riding together?

The Outlaw as Martyr

THOSE WERE THE DAYS when the Americans in the Philippines were beginning to enjoy "the Islands" and its people. And on their part the Filipinos—at least the educated ones—were having a taste of that milk of American kindness called "Benevolent Assimilation." The *americanos* were making civil service more efficient and more suitable for "little brown brother." They phased out those old-fashioned, horse-drawn vehicles to make way for modern electric cars. They drained the canals and the moats and the *esteros*, and improved the water systems to combat cholera and all those other dreaded plagues. And the famous landscape architect, D.H. Burnham, was here to make Manila—and yes, Baguio—truly beautiful.

William Howard Taft's tongue-in-cheek slogan "The Philippines for the Filipinos!" was the order of the day. Filipino elders like Pardo de Tavera were *delegados* to the St. Louis Expositions. Filipino boys like Osias were *pensionados* in Washington. Smaller kids like Tomas Claudio were growing into a whole generation of "sajones," as Nick Joaquin aptly calls them, who can't wait to fight America's wars for democracy. The proverbial Maria Clara girl was coming out of her timid *terno*—faking it as some little Asiatic "Gibson girl"—sporting western garb, speech, and monicker. And "schoolmarms" like Ada Avelino (Librada to the old school) would be teaching turn-of-the-century Filipinos and Americans alike what should be taught about the Philippines— said she (according to Gregorio F. Zaide) to Prescott F. Jernegan, another American who "wrote" Philippine history, when he

103

called Aguinaldo the "chief of the Cavite bandits": "Mr. Jernegan, Aguinaldo was not a bandit. Our revolutionists were not bandits. They were patriots just like the Americans who revolted against England in 1776." But in the classrooms where "Ma'am Ada" taught, giant pictures of Lincoln and Washington stared down on Filipino boys and girls who sang the Star-Spangled Banner, recited Whitman and Longfellow, and enjoyed recess drinking Coke.

Those were the heydays for the pioneers of 20th century Filipino talent. The *Banda Pasig* and the *Banda Arevalo* were waltzing or marching with honors under the magnificent baton of Maestro Ladislao Bonus. Severino Reyes and his patriotic *zarzuelas* were taking over the colonial *moro-moros*. The "Great Tenor" Victorino Carrion and "showbiz" queens Yeyeng Fernandez and Estanislawa San Miguel (was she related to the Hero of 1903?) were singing their way into the hearts of native and foreign Manileños at the Teatro Zorilla. Fabian de la Rosa, the painter, would carry on the Luna tradition to win a gold medal at the St. Louis Exposition. Fernando Canon, the ex-*insurrecto* general, would carry on his battles at the Barcelona International Chess Tournament.

But this was the benevolent side of assimilation; its reverse side was far from wholesome. In the far South, the "monkeys who have no tails" hadn't knuckled under Old Glory yet; they hadn't stopped "running amok," to use an American G.I. phrase originated from the Moro wars. In Samar, the "howling wilderness" of Lukban's time, the *Pulahanes* were still as fiery as the red pants they wore. In Central Luzon, the Santa Iglesia continued to "evangelize" the peasants in the plains with cross and sword. In the Bilibid, Ricarte the Vibora remained unconquered even in the loneliness of his solitary cell. And in Tagalog *bosque* country, *Supremo* Sakay and his *Katagalugan* guerrillas had suddenly become active again during the last half of 1904 and the first quarter of 1905.

James H. Blount, in his *The American Occupation of the Philippines,* refers to this last-mentioned activity as "the Cavite-Batangas-Laguna insurrection." And he quotes portions of the *Philippine Commission Report* for 1905 for the causes that led to its outbreak:

In the autumn of 1904 it became necessary to withdraw a number of the constabulary from these provinces to assist in suppressing disorder which had broken out in the province of Samar. . . .

There was at the time [the fall of 1904] also considerable activity among the small group of irreconcilables in Manila, who began agitating for immediate independence, doubtless because of the supposed effect it would have on the presidential election in the United States, in which the Philippines was a large topic of discussion. Evidently this was regarded as a favorable time for demonstration by Felizardo, Montalon, de Vega, Oruga, Sakay [etc.]. *These men had been officers of the Filipino army during the insurrection.* (Brackets and underscoring by Blount)

"Montalon," as the Americans got used to misspelling his name, was the overall chief of operations of the *Katagalugan* forces. But it was Felizardo who among the guerrilla leaders was "the most active"—in the words of Colonel David Baker, who later crushed Montalan's forces with ruthless and sometimes inhuman methods. And until Felizardo was finally tracked down and murdered in March 1906 by Constabulary *secretas* who infiltrated his band, he would indeed give the *constabularios*, the scouts, and their American masters the worries of their lives. Among his more famous raids were those of San Pedro Tunasan (Laguna) on 12 November 1904 and of Parañaque, very near Manila, on 8 December of that year. In this last raid, his men came into town dressed in captured Constabulary tunics and they carted away some 20 guns and boxes of ammunition, while the greater part of the garrison was attending a fiesta in another town.

"Felizardo was remarkable for his audacity, his fine horsemanship, and his expert marksmanship," writes the Englishman John Foreman in *The Philippine Islands*. And Foreman tells how, during the Parañaque attack, mounted on "a beautiful pony stolen from the race-track of Pasay," General Felizardo "rode swiftly past a constabulary sentinel, who shot at him and missed, whilst Felizardo from his seat in the saddle, shot the sentinel dead."

Elsewhere, *Katagalugan* fighters were not to be outdone. Also in December 1904, Colonel Masigla fought a detachment of Constabulary in Alfonso (Cavite), while Colonel de Vega ambushed another enemy force at a place called Marquina near the Cavite-Batangas border. Joining forces later, de Vega and Masigla crossed over to Batangas and with Colonel Bito attacked Taal on 5 January 1905. This time they carried away 35 guns from the local constabulary and police forces, and P15,000 from the municipal treasury of Taal. General Aniceto Oruga raided Talisay on his own on the 12th of January, losing one of his commanders. All these movements pointed to a concentration of forces on the Tagaytay mountain ridge, where Montalan's headquarters was located, and the reason for this became clear when, on 25 January, General Julian Montalan personally led all the various guerrilla bands under his overall command in a mass assault on his own hometown of San Francisco de Malabon.

For the U.S. Philippine Commission, this was the last straw that prompted it to authorize the declaration of martial law and to resort again to reconcentration methods as was done before against Lukban, Malvar, Ola, and others. And for *Katagalugan*, this would be the last stand that ended in the weakening of its anti-American resistance. Among those captured was Oruga, the "terror" of Laguna and Batangas. And among those killed was the slippery and mysterious Felizardo of Cavite.

Revolutionary movements, it is said, have to terminate in two ways. One is when it has succeeded in overthrowing the existing authority, and the other if it is liquidated. The 1903-1907 Philippine model led by Sakay ended in the latter way, its libertarian fire extinguished by the compromise idea of a "National Assembly."

Sakay was tricked into submission through this proposal—and then hanged. But his willingness to lay down his arms was in good faith, solicited by the *ilustrado* politicos who were themselves involved in the nationalist movement, and inspired by the conditions set forth by the United States government for the establishment of the First National Assembly.

Recall that the "Philippine Bill" passed by the U.S. Congress in 1902 set two conditions for the creation of this Assembly: first, the publication of a Philippine census; and then, the complete restoration of peace. The census was completed and published in March 1905. Next, the provinces—except Isabela, Samar, and Cavite—held elections for municipal officials in December of that year, and for provincial governors in February 1906. The disturbances in Isabela and Samar were subsequently put down by American armed might. But the *Katagalugan* movement persisted in Cavite, showed no signs of relenting and had, in fact, threatened to spread anew. What happened next was the paradox of the entire drama of those first few years of the American occupation of the Philippines.

The role of mediator and, perhaps, unknowing tool of the American authorities was taken by Dr. Dominador Gomez. This remnant of the *ilustrado* propaganda movement of the 1880s had in the 1900s surfaced again as a political agitator. Gomez was, in fact, a rabid nationalist agitator who went in and out of prison for his rabble-rousing activities. He and Isabelo de los Reyes were the fathers of the *obrero* movement that was born in the midst of the Malvar, San Miguel, and Sakay struggles; and it was he who had tried to save the Partido Nacionalista from disintegrating when Poblete and Sakay were imprisoned, by taking over its presidency and, through that body, directing the guerrilla bands holding out in the hills, including *Katagalugan*. His mediation efforts in 1906, now that there was a promise of a "national assembly" from America, must therefore be understood as a political option—an extension of his own persuasion which was, understandably enough, typically *ilustrado*.

After the ban on political agitation was lifted and political parties other than the Federalistas were permitted to organize again, for the purpose of elections, Gomez restructured the outlawed Partido Nacionalista into the *Partido Popular Independista*—at a time when Sakay was up in arms, Poblete was still in jail, and Alvarez was nowhere in sight. Of several pro-independence parties, the Partido Popular was the "only advocate of immediate independence without American intervention of any kind," in the words of David Barrows. The word "Popular" was added to proclaim its mass base, as well as to distinguish it from two other "independista" parties: the *Partido Independista* formed by the inevitable Pedro Paterno late in 1902 (which was really nothing but a splinter group of the Federal Party) and the recently formed *Partido Independista Inmediata* led by Quezon, Osmeña, and their kind. And yet, in the end, even a "radical organization" (again, words by Barrows) such as the Gomez party would accept compromise and, to use a modern phraseology, co-optate for the sellout concept of the Philippine Assembly.

American writers like Barrows later alleged that the new American Governor-General, Henry C. Ide, while giving authority for Gomez to negotiate, was "careful to stipulate that no terms were to be offered [to Sakay] and that the surrender should be unconditional." But letters exchanged between Gomez and Sakay, published in *Muling Pagsilang* and later reproduced by Jose P. Santos and Antonio K. Abad in their works, reveal the duplicity of the American intention, as proven by events subsequent to the surrender negotiations.

Sakay came down to Manila on 14 July 1906. He had agreed to make final negotiations with the American authorities after preliminary conferences with Dr. Gomez at his *Di-Masalang* mountain headquarters in Tanay. To show his sincerity, the *Presidente Supremo* of the Republic of *Katagalugan* brought along his entire military staff, including Carreon, Montalan, and Villafuerte. The American Provost Marshall's office in Manila provided them the necessary safe-conduct pass.

The outcome of these negotiations remain a mystery. More perplexing was the manner in which the Constabulary later "captured" Sakay and his officers. According to Francisco Carreon's testimony, the *Katagalugan* leaders came to Manila four times. The fatal fourth time led to their arrest—and to Sakay's death.

It seems that their safe-conduct pass was good only for Manila and back to Tanay. Naively on their part or simply out of good faith, perhaps, Sakay and his companions accepted an invitation from an old foe, Colonel Louis Van Schaick, then acting Governor of Cavite, to attend a *baile* in their honor, celebrating their acceptance of peace. General Leon Villafuerte, who lived until the 1950s, vividly recalled this event to Antonio Abad in these words:

> We arrived at 10 a.m. in Cavite in uniforms, with our daggers and pistols, accompanied by Captains Winfield Scott Grove and Rafael Crame, and Dr. Dominador Gomez. The *Estado Mayor* of General Sakay were all together except for General Francisco Carreon who was left in Manila because of illness. The building was well decorated with American flags and beautiful flowers. There was also an orchestra playing. But the most interesting of all were some beautiful ladies, including American women, who were present at the banquet. When the orchestra struck up the first notes we were invited to dance. Benito Natividad (not the revolutionary general from Nueva Ecija), Gregorio Porto, Isabelo Despida and Felix Atanacio, junior officers of our band . . . were dancing. Only Macario Sakay and Julian Montalan did not join the dance; they were in one corner of the hall. It seems to me that they really disliked mingling with the new masters of our country. I took for my partner the pretty daughter of Governor Van Schaick. . . .

The unsuspecting *guerrilleros* were in the middle of a dance when the Cavite Constabulary suddenly cordoned the place in full battle gear and with fixed bayonets. Captain Grove succeeded in disarming Sakay who, says Villafuerte, "fought unarmed against his giant attacker." Montalan was the first to sense trouble and with revolver drawn he readied himself for a fight. Villafuerte and de Vega, when they realized what was happening, left their partners in the middle of the dance hall to join the rest of the group on the side of Sakay, covering with their guns everybody in the reception room. But at this point, according to Villafuerte, Dr. Gomez once again employed his diplomacy on Sakay and his officers who—"convinced of the hopelessness of the situation"—finally surrendered their weapons. When Grove came to him, Villafuerte says he unloaded his revolver and threw it to a corner, telling the American officer to get it himself. Villafuerte's narrative continues:

Papers for us to sign were next brought out. Obviously, the party to where we were invited was a downright ruse after all, a clever plan to trap us inside enemy territory, far from the danger of inciting popular disfavor. [What Villafuerte meant here was that it would have been an entirely different story had this treachery happened in Manila.]

We were told that the papers dealt merely with an acceptance of the proposed national assembly and that there was nothing to worry about being death warrants. I knew they meant the opposite.

General Villafuerte's suspicions were well-founded. Later during their trial proceedings, the prosecution produced a document signed by them—and incriminating them all. Here's a full text of that paper as it appeared in the *Report of the Philippine Commission* for the year 1907:

BUREAU OF CONSTABULARY, INFORMATION DIVISION.
OFFICE OF THE SUPERINTENDENT.
MANILA, P.I.

PHILIPPINE ISLANDS,
Cavite Province, Luzon, ss:

Personally appeared before me, the undersigned, Macario Sakay, Julian Montalon [*sic*], Leon Villafuerte, Lucio de Vega and Benito Natividad who, being duly sworn according to law, deposed the following:

That they have surrendered to Col. H.H. Bandholtz, of the Constabulary, voluntarily and without promises, conditions, or offers of any class having been made except just and legal treatment, and understanding that they are to appear before a competent court there to answer for the acts committed by them in the field; that the actual reasons for their surrender have been that the person who have [sic] arranged same have convinced them that their stay in the field was prejudicial to the interests of the country, whereas their surrender would be of great benefit; that this statement is free and spontaneous, without being their prisoners or in detention, and without any kind of imprisonment or violence, and for the sole purpose that there may be no doubts or misinterpretation in regard to the motives that they may have inspired this act.

                         Macario Sakay.
                         Julian Montalon (his "X" mark).
                         L.D. Villafuerte.
                         Lucio de Vega.
                         Benito Natividad.

Witnesses:

L.J. VAN SCHAICK
    Governor of Cavite.
DOMI[NA]DOR GOMEZ.
CHARLES F. HERR
    First Lieutenant, Twenty-first Inf.

Subscribed and sworn to before me this 17th day of July 1906.

                         SULPICIO ANTONI.
                         Acting Provincial Secretary, Cavite.

[Captains Winfield S. Grove and Rafael Crame signed as witnesses to the "X" signature of Julian Montalan.]

General Sakay and his officers, heavily guarded and manacled, were brought back to Manila as prisoners. After a few days their trials began, which brought them to various places in Rizal, Bulacan, Laguna, Batangas, and Cavite where the crimes charged against them were committed. The principal charge was "bandolerismo" (brigandage), punishable by death under the

110

Bandolerismo Act of 1902. Judge Ignacio Villamor presided over the court. Fiscal Francisco Santa Maria was prosecutor. Attorneys Felipe Buencamino, Sr., Ramon Diokno and Julian Gerona (a former Guam deportee) were lawyers for the defense.

On 6 August 1907, Judge Villamor sentenced Macario Sakay, Francisco Carreon, Julian Montalan, Leon Villafuerte, and Lucio de Vega to be hanged until dead for the crime of "bandolerismo." Although their surrender and initial trial had taken place during the term of Governor-General Henry C. Ide, the authority to review and commute their cases passed to Ide's successor, James F. Smith, who confirmed the death sentence on Sakay and de Vega, and commuted those of the others to life imprisonment at the Bilibid.

On 13 September 1907, Sakay and de Vega were hanged. Till their last moments, they proclaimed their patriotism: *"Mga tunay na Katipunan kami!"*

The fond memory of 1907 had been "our First Philippine Assembly," of which Dominador Gomez was one of the elected delegates. Next-generation Filipinos would remember the day it was inaugurated on 16 October as a "milestone" that paved the way for our "political maturity" and "independence." But those who see 1907 from another perspective see it mainly as a year of final nationalist suppression. In reality, 1907 signifies two events we have been trained to forget: the banning of the Filipino flag on 23 August, and the killing of General Sakay on 13 September.

The Americans hanged Macario Sakay for banditry. But those hip to the politics and rhetorics of the early 1900s see this happening not as a defamation of the man, but as a glorification of the gallows. The late Teodoro Agoncillo, for one, had always insisted that the Americans and their *americanistas* liquidated the "last of the guerrilla patriots."

Or was it the first Huk?

PICTORIAL ESSAY

KATAGALUGAN was, to Andres Bonifacio, both the *Haring Bayan* (Tondo), the *Kataastaasang Kapulungan* or Supreme Council of the Katipunan—and the *Inang Bayan* (Filipinas), the Sovereign Nation of the Sons of the People. *Kalayaan* of the *Inang Bayan*, under the aegis of the *Haring Bayan*, was the supreme ideal of all "*tunay na* Katipunan"—those crusading *true* Katipuneros who had worked so hard since 1892 for the cause of brotherhood and freedom, as epitomized by the great triumvirate of plebeian hero-martyrs from the "Tagalog center" of Tondo: Andres Bonifacio "Maypag-asa," Emilio Jacinto "Pingkian," and Macario Sakay "Dapitan." All three followed only the Light of *their* Katipunan, leading heroic and tragic lives, in the end dying for their revolutionary convictions. Bonifacio died at the hands of "brothers" in Cavite in 1897. Jacinto died in lonely isolation somewhere in Laguna in 1899. And Sakay died by an American hangman's noose in Bilibid in 1907.

**ANDRES BONIFACIO
"MAYPAG-ASA"**

**MACARIO SAKAY
"DAPITAN"**

**EMILIO JACINTO
"PINGKIAN"**

GEN. ARTEMIO RICARTE
"VIBORA"

GEN. SANTIAGO ALVAREZ
"APOY"

GEN. LUCIANO SAN MIGUEL

GEN. EMILIO AGUINALDO
"MAGDALO"

GEN. PANTALEON GARCIA

GEN. PIO DEL PILAR

FACTIONS of the Katipunan in 1896 in Cavite were the *Magdiwang* of Noveleta, led by the Alvarezes, and the *Magdalo* of Kawit, led by the Aguinaldos. Among the *Magdiwangs* were Artemio Ricarte "Vibora," Mariano Trias, the Riego de Dios brothers, Luciano San Miguel, and Julian Montalan. Allied to *Magdalo* were Vito Belarmino, Mariano Noriel, Tomas Mascardo, Pantaleon Garcia, Agapito Bonzon, and the Tirona brothers. Pio del Pilar's *Magtagumpay* group from Makati favored Aguinaldo's side (as did other Manileños like Edilberto Evangelista and Feliciano Jocson). *Magdiwang* sided for a while with the *Supremo*'s *Katagalugan* of Tondo. But in the end, by the middle of 1897, *Magdiwang* united with *Magdalo* in favor of a republican government, and the *Haring Bayan* became the proverbial outsider in that clan war between the Cavite factions. From then on until 1902, the Revolution would bear the stamp of *Magdalo*'s (and Emilio Aguinaldo's) "cavitismo."

MALOLOS 1898: *VIVA* **TO THE LIBERATING REPUBLICAN ARMY**

SANTA MESA 1899: LUCIANO SAN MIGUEL AS *REPUBLICANO* **IN WORD WAR WITH NEBRASKAN COL. JOHN STOTSENBURG**

SAMAR 1902: LUKBAN'S GUERRILLAS
SURRENDER IN CATUBIG

MALVAR OF BATANGAS

REPUBLICANOS were born out of the *Magdalo-Magdiwang* union in the *ilustrado*-dominated Tejeros Assembly of 1897 that repudiated the Katipunan and liquidated its *Supremo*. The Republic that in 1898 declared Philippine independence at Kawit—and assembled a national congress at Malolos, where Emilio Aguinaldo's government had its national seat—later went to war as a national response to American aggression. Though its army was largely peasant-based, its leadership was principally bourgeois: first under Antonio Luna, then under Aguinaldo himself, and finally under Miguel Malvar. The "insurrection" that broke out in February 1899 near Santa Mesa, in General San Miguel's zone, was officially declared over by the Americans in mid-1902, after ruthless "pacification" campaigns decimated the republican "insurrecto" hold-outs of General Lukban in Samar, General Guevarra in Leyte, General Noriel in Cavite, and—the "last"—General Malvar in Batangas.

**THE PHILIPPINE CONSTABULARY
UNDER THE AMERICANS**

**MACABEBES: THE ORIGINAL
PHILIPPINE SCOUTS**

IMPERIALIST victory over Emilio Aguinaldo's *republica* did not end the Revolution. After 1902, U.S. "benevolent assimilation" took the form of "pacifying" Filipinos still up in arms against their own brother Filipinos. The Philippine Scouts and the Philippine Constabulary were recruited, armed, drilled, paid, fed, and led by the American masters to hunt down and exterminate born-again *Katipuneros* who kept up the anti-American resistance abandoned by the *ilustrado* generals of the Republic. Ex-General Licerio Geronimo in Rizal, ex-Colonel Agapito Bonzon in Cavite, and ex-General Nicolas Gonzales in Batangas were among those sworn in as *constabulario* inspectors for the Southern Tagalog region. The justification for their acts was, of course, that they were not fighting former comrades in the Revolution—i.e., "genuine *revolucionarios*"—but *only* Katipuneros condemned by the American colonial government as well as by the first Philippine Republic.

P.C. CHIEF HENRY T. ALLEN

P.C. INSPECTOR
AGAPITO BONZON

P.C. CAPTAIN CARY CROCKETT

BANDOLERISMO was the "crime" for which many unsurrendered post-Malvar patriots were outlawed—and condemned—by the Americans. Branded as "bandoleros" were such fighters as Faustino Guillermo, Julian Santos, Benito Santa Ana, Apolonio Samson, and Ciriaco Contreras who all fought in General San Miguel's "bandit" army; as well as Francisco Carreon, Julian Montalan, Cornelio Felizardo, Aniceto Oruga, Leon Villafuerte, Cosme Caro, and Lucio de Vega who served in General Sakay's *Republika ng Katagalugan*. Colonial authorities saw to it that the Sedition Law of 1901 and the Bandolerismo Act of 1902 were made especially effective in suppressing these radical nationalist movements—and such other "ladrones" as the Ricartistas, the Salvadoristas, the Colorums, the Babaylanes, the Pulahanes, and the Moros of Mindanao. Not armed might, however, but the appeal for peace of the *politicos* and the elite-incited clamor for a "national assembly" finally weakened guerrilla resistance by 1907.

**GEN. FAUSTINO GUILLERMO;
THE "JUNGLE FOX" CAPTURED**

**GEN. JULIAN MONTALAN:
SAVED BY *ANTING-ANTING*?**

**COL. LUCIO DE VEGA:
HANGED BY THE AMERICANS**

POST-"BANDOLERO" DAYS IN A CAVITE TOWN

THE AMERICAN-SPONSORED
"FIRST PHILIPPINE ASSEMBLY" OF 1907

HANGINGS made heroes and martyrs of the most radical and most aggressive of the post-Malvar guerrilla leaders. The San Miguelista general, Faustino Guillermo, captured by P.C. *secretas* in 1903 and charged with "bandolerismo," was hanged in Pasig in 1904. *Katagalugan*'s *Supremo* Macario Sakay and Colonel Lucio de Vega, subdued through another deception in 1906 and also condemned as "bandoleros," were hanged together at the Bilibid in 1907. And many more patriots called bandits before and after them contributed their names to a long list of unsung and unremembered—even vilified—fighters of a belittled anti-imperialist war who all brought glory to the gallows: Rumbaoa, Rosales, Gutierrez, Celedonio, Angeles, Frani, del Prado, Infante, Rios, Tomines, Salvador, Noriel, and others. On these pages are typical hanging scenes in the Philippines in those early American "empire days."

A TYPICAL HANGING SCENE

AMERICAN HANGMEN AT THE OLD BILIBID GAT

A DOUBLE HANGING SCENE

A TRIPLE HANGING SCENE

SURVIVORS of the "bandit" wars were few. The true Katipunero Francisco Carreon spent the best years of his life in Bilibid, but felt no pain for the "treachery" of Dominador Gomez whom he cleared in 1930 of any guilt regarding his (and Sakay's) sad fate. In contrast Artemio Ricarte the Vibora harbored such hatred for America that he returned from exile in the 1940s to "liberate" his *Inang Bayan with* the Japanese. Julian Montalan, the legend, who survived 10 years of exile/ imprisonment at hard labor in Iwahig (where he later married a rich Chinese trader's heiress) was—by then—dead. But Leon Villafuerte, the frustrated *marino*, lived on to the 1950s (as did Ola of Albay) to tell Antonio K. Abad the story of how he fought with Sakay—refuting the charge of banditry by Americans and their *americanistas*. And Gorio Porto was still around in the 1960s, dictating to a nephew the testament of his (and Montalan's) patriotism—and exciting readers with tales (yarns?) of "treasures" buried by Cavite's peasant hero.

THE "PEACE TIME" VILLAFUERTE

FRANCISCO CARREON (RIGHT) WITH FELLOW KATIPUNAN/KATAGALUGAN *VETERANOS* BRICCIO PANTAS, VALENTIN DIAZ, AND PIO VALENZUELA

EPILOGUE

AFTER SAN MIGUEL'S DEATH in 1903, his group—"one of the largest and most formidable bands thus formed," according to the Watson papers—was reduced to splinters led by Faustino Guillermo, Tomas de Guzman, Ciriaco Contreras, Apolonio Samson, and Leon Villafuerte. One by one, the first four leaders were cornered, killed, or hanged. The surviving fifth, Villafuerte of Bulacan, would join Sakay's *Katagalugan*.

After Ricarte's capture in 1904, his earlier agitations appear to have fructified. Felipe Salvador whom he sought out in Nueva Ecija and commissioned a major-general, led his Santa Iglesia guerrillas in a number of raids in various parts of Central Luzon. Manuel Tomines, whom Ricarte appointed a colonel, led a revolt in Isabela together with the American "insurrecto" Major Maurice Sibley. And Sakay, with whom the Vibora differed on questions of leadership and strategy, activated his forces anyway and so greatly alarmed the American authorities they had to declare martial law (with the writ of *habeas corpus* suspended) and reintroduced the *zona* system in the Tagalog provinces south of Manila. (Tomines was hanged in 1905, Sakay in 1907, and Salvador in 1910.)

After Sakay's capture in 1906, the old Katipunan radicals of the Partido Nacionalista that had one way or another backed up the unsurrendered guerrillas, again called for a secret meeting in Quiapo, where they had first met in 1901. Only five responded to this call, and the Watson papers gave the explanation that "most of the former leaders were either serving sentence in the Bilibid or had been hanged for their crimes, or were still out in the field." The five diehards who came, at any rate, united the plural elements of the Revolution. Pascual Poblete, a crusading journalist with socialist leanings, was a leftover (together with Isabelo de los Reyes and

Dominador Gomez, now his colleagues in the *obrero* movement) of the Propaganda movement in Europe whose attacks on Spanish colonialism shifted to tirades against American imperialism—through the nationalist paper, *El Grito del Pueblo*. Valentin Diaz, of peasant Ilocano stock, was one of the founding members of the Katipunan and an active Freemason curiously linked to the politico-religious activities of the Guardia de Honor, Santa Iglesia, and Aglipayano movements. Santiago Alvarez, of the Cavite gentry, was generalissimo of the *Magdiwang* Army of the Cavite Katipunan in 1896, and the "Quiapo Assembly" that founded the Partido Nacionalista in 1901 elected him its first president. Alberto Bautista was of the younger, wealthier crop of 1899 (he fought in Ilocos with the famous Tinio Brigade) who was "katipunized," *republicano*-style, when he fought with Tomines in Isabela until 1901. And Pantaleon Torres represented *Katagalugan*, that hard core of Tondo revolutionaries epitomized by the great triumvirate of Bonifacio, Jacinto, and Sakay.

Meanwhile, the Santa Iglesia members began calling themselves "Salvadoristas" after their leader. And during 1906, the Salvadoristas as such raided Malolos.

While Sakay and his associate, Lucio de Vega, hanged at the Bilibid in 1907, crying out *"Mga tunay na Katipunan kami!"* before their *berdugos* noosed them, Ricarte in his cell block (he had been sentenced to solitary confinement) kept busy "making *pactos de sangre* (blood compacts) . . . organizing another political society." The plan was said to have been smuggled out of prison and delivered to a certain Tiburcio in Mariveles.

Meanwhile, the Salvadoristas were getting the brunt of the Constabulary's "clean-up"drives. After a minor encounter on 24 June 1910, Felipe Salvador was finally captured.

While "Apo Ipe" awaited his own execution, Ricarte went out of prison on 26 June—not a bit less radical than when he first came in six years before. The Americans exiled him again to Hongkong, where he was to stay until 1915.

While Ricarte was getting older in Hongkong, the nationalist movement back home was also reverting to pluralism and sectarianism. There were Salvadoristas, Rizalistas, Aglipayanos, Katipuneros and, of course, Ricartistas—all acting on their own, fighting foreign and native imperialism while fighting each other.

As the Constabulary hunt for the remnants of the Santa Iglesia went on, another *iglesia* leader, Aglipayano Simeon Mandac (the suspended governor of Ilocos Norte who had once been an anti-American guerrilla commander under Padre Aglipay) was himself hunted for leading a revolt in Nueva Vizcaya (which did not succeed) in September 1910.

Between 1911 and 1914, Rufino Vicente, Juan Evangelista, Modesto Victorino, Brigido Santiago, and Timoteo Carriaga—all well-known Ricartistas—created disturbances in Manila and Rizal and tried to activate other provinces in Luzon as well as in the Visayas. Secret societies bearing such mysterious names as Di-*Masalang, Mapagsumikap, Makabuhay, Pagkakaisa,* and *Anak-Bayan* sowed discord among peasants and urban workers against the American colonial regime. (Some of the leaders were old Katipuneros, like *Di-Masalang's* Patricio Belen and *Makabuhay's* Santiago Alvarez.) Four attempted revolutions involving these and other societies occurred during this period: the so-called Fourth of July and Balintawak plots of 1912, and the Balintawak and Christmas Eve plots of 1914.

By 1915, the Revolution to which all these movements claimed continuity was just a memory which no one but Ricarte alone now perhaps believed in and still wished to continue—and finish. As the ex-*insurrecto* Manuel Luis Quezon, who would become president of the Commonwealth, spoke for himself in his memoirs: "By this time even the most intransigent Filipinos, with the exception of General Ricarte . . . had become sincere friends and loyal supporters of the United States." The era of suppressed nationalism was about to end because, by the next decade, that generation of Filipinos would be overwhelmingly "sajonista"—American-lovers always itching to fight and die for America's "wars for democracy" (remember Tomas Claudio and his ilk?) and always raring to lobby in the U.S. mainland with the "independence missions" (remember OSROX and all that?).

The old radicals of the Katipunan and the Partido Nacionalista had aged and mellowed—if they were not already dead. Poblete was approaching his 60s. Tolentino had passed on (to another incarnation?) in 1911. Gomez, de los Reyes, Lope K. Santos, and other patriots-turned-*politicos* were by now bureaucrats themselves. And the younger crop of nationalists were becoming more and more attracted to a new brand of radicalism: the socialist struggle.

127

The 1920s and 1930s saw the emergence of the doctrinaire social movements: the *Tanggulan* of Patricio Dionisio, the *Sakdalista* of Benigno Ramos, the *Partido Socialista* of Pedro Abad Santos, and the *Partido Komunista* of Crisanto Evangelista. The links with the Revolution were still there: the *Socialista* "Don Perico" Abad Santos had been an officer under that 1901 Guam deportee and hero General Hizon; the *Sakdalista* Nicolas Encallado had fought in the army of that 1902 Batangas holdout General Malvar; and Hermenegildo Cruz, the *Marxista*, had been a printer for the revolutionary newspapers.

But these "neo-Katipunans" had nothing in common with Ricarte now, except that they shared his anti-American sentiment. The contradiction now lies, in fact, in Ricarte himself. Having been given asylum in Japan for most of his expatriate years, he naturally came to love the Japanese people as his own. For this, Ricarte would find himself in a rather uncomfortable position when the Pacific war broke out, because the anti-imperialist movements that should have been closest to his heart were also *anti*-Japanese. The Second World War thus found the various anti-imperialist movements, peasant or *ilustrado*, either joining Ricarte's MAKAPILI or Abad Santos-Evangelista's HUKBALAHAP.

And, of course, fighting on the side of the old enemy, the *americanos*, were the "americanized" children and grandchildren of '96, '99 and the early 1900s—our own fathers and elder brothers whose fathers and grandfathers before them died in the battlefields, in prisons, on the scaffolds, and in national memory in an earlier war which American "benevolence" had made them forget. Truly, by then, its own children had devoured the Revolution.

To a generation of Filipinos who grew up venerating without understanding Rizal or Bonifacio, quoting Whitman and Longfellow without even knowing Balagtas or Batute, and colonializing their own native tastes with foxtrot and Coke, the likes of Ricarte, San Miguel, Montalan, Sakay, et al. were until the 1960s still bandits and outlaws and crackpots and opportunists. Efforts of nationalist historians to enlighten us on our miseducation almost led—but not quite—to their canonization as heroes in the 1970s.

Instead, born-again San Miguels, Montalans, and Sakays moved with the green brown multitude to become new Bandoleros . . .

AUTHOR'S NOTES

MY VERY FIRST EXPOSURE to "bandit" history was Antonio K. Abad's *General Macario L. Sakay: Was He a Bandit or a Patriot?* (1955), which I found in one of those old bookstores on that Manila main street once called Azcarraga and which I bought for one peso and fifty centavos out of my meager high school allowance in the late 1950s. Had I chosen to stroll along neighboring Raon, that much money could have gone instead to a 45-rpm Elvis or Little Richard record—or to a Harvey Kurtzman-edited vintage MAD comicbook, had I headed for the newsstands on Avenida Rizal.

My abrupt defection from rock-n-roll and Kurtzmania, and sudden shift to "Filipiniana"—horribly corny stuff in those days—began from a reading (and subsequent pride of ownership) of Gregorio Zaide's *The Philippine Revolution* (1954) in one of those then popular Vasquez book stores. *Ganoon ba?* was my own reaction for Zaide's "illuminating" names and dates—and whatever he may have said and done (or didn't) before and after, Zaide had surely been one of the strong influence in leading me away from Hollywood movies and Classics Illustrated. Graduating later on to Teodoro Agoncillo's classic *Revolt of the Masses* (1956) I was, by now, already looking back—long before Ambeth Ocampo could even see the light—at "bandit" periodical literature: Vicente Barranco's "He Fought with Sakay" (*Sunday Times Magazine,* 1946), Abelardo Mojica's "The Surrender of Macario Sakay" (*This Week Magazine,* 1950), Armando J. Malay's "The Sakay Republic" (*Weekly Women's Magazine,* 1957), and Gregorio Porto's "Buried Treasures Lie Untouched in Cavite" (*Manila Times Daily Magazine,* 1960).

By the 1960s I had no more qualms about the "bandits"—Sakay, Ola, Montalan, *et al.*—being really authentic heroes whose responses

129

to U.S. imperialism may have been harsh and uncivil, true, but were nevertheless motivated by staunch patriotism and nationalism far greater than that of any of those compromising leaders of the fallen first Philippine Republic. A decade after Abad's *Sakay,* college requirements as a Fine Arts student at the University of Santo Tomas led me to do research at the neighboring Sampaloc Public Library—now vacated—where serendipity rewarded me with the delightful discovery of Vic Hurley's *Jungle Patrol* (New York, 1935) in the library's Filipiniana shelves. *Jungle Patrol,* subtitled "The Story of the Philippine Constabulary," seemed to be unwanted by historians of that generation apparently because it didn't read like the usual history books. But for me, it was a welcome introduction to a Luciano San Miguel I had never known in Kalaw's, Zaide's, Agoncillo's or any other Filipino historian's work before the 1970s, and it led me to further researches on this particular unaccepted hero—culminating with my 1965 article, "Gen. Luciano San Miguel: A Rebel to the End," in the *Mirror Magazine.* I am indebted to Hurley's book (now available as a Filipiniana Reprint Series of Solar Books) for teaching me the art of reading between the lines, and finding hidden insights of Filipino patriotism and heroism beneath the bias of American colonial accounts.

Going back to Antonio Abad's *Sakay,* I must say it was a badly printed, badly organized, and not-so-well-written book. But it made up in sincerity and candor for which I had always admired its author, as much as I had always respected another non-scholar student of history, the illustrious Jose Paez Santos, whose own much earlier work, *Tatlong Napabantog na "Tulisan" sa Pilipinas* (1935), I would only discover two decades later after a reading of Renato Constantino's footnotes in his *The Philippines: A Past Revisited* (1976).

But somehow, to me, the key to full enlightenment on "bandit" history still seemed to be missing—until I thought Reynaldo C. Ileto provided *that* key in his *Pasyon and Revolution* (1977). Historians before him (including even Agoncillo and Constantino) missed the whole point of the post-1902 resistance when they wrote of Sakay's "Tagalog Republic"—it was a misnomer and it was meaningless. Ileto it was who finally used the proper term—*Ang Republica ng Katagalugan*—and using that term made it so easy for him (as it did for me) to see Sakay's struggle in legitimate affinity to Bonifacio's and Jacinto's labors, and as easy to defend Sakay from the charges of "bandolerismo" from both Americans and pro-American Filipinos.

Needless to say, this present work owes much in insight to Ileto's *Pasyon*, without which the perspectives for my *"Bandoleros"* would never have been drawn the way they were. And, in turn, the late missionary prophet William Henry Scott, who came as a teacher when this pupil was ready, helped draw and polish these perspectives with his appreciation, criticisms, and encouragement. He passed away without seeing *our* Bandoleros ride again in this book as the people's heroes they truly were, but he and them must certainly be now comrades in the Otherwhere.

FOR LUCIANO SAN MIGUEL, I consulted mainly the memoirs of Aguinaldo (*Reseña*), Alejandrino, Alvarez, (Pio) del Pilar, Ricarte and Quintos; Agoncillo's *Revolt of the Masses* and *Malolos: Crisis of the Republic*, Baclagon's *Philippine Campaigns*, Constantino's *The Philippines: A Past Revisited*, Devins' *An Observer in the Philippines*, Faust's *Campaigning in the Philippines*, Hurley's *Jungle Patrol*, Kalaw's *The Philippine Revolution*, Scott's monographs on Isabelo de los Reyes and the *Union Obrera Democratica*, Willis' *Our Philippine Problem*, Wolff's *Little Brown Brother*, and Zaide's *The Philippine Revolution;* the manuscript collection in the National Library Filipiniana Division known as "Philippine Insurgent Records" (sometimes called the *"insurrecto* papers") and Taylor's five-volume printed work based on these documents; the U.S. Philippine Commission *Annual Report* for 1903; and my own "Rebel to the End" and "Himagsikan ng mga Tulisan."

For Julian Montalan, my principal sources were the memoirs of Aguinaldo (*Gunita*), Alvarez, Porto (as told to a nephew in a magazine article) and Ricarte; Abad's *General Macario L. Sakay,* Agoncillo's *Revolt*, Barranco's "He Fought with Sakay," Barrows' *History of the Philippines*, Blount's *The American Occupation of the Philippines*, Cabrera's "Macario Sakay," Castillo's "The Life and Times of a Minor Myth" and "The Revolution in Cavite," Constantino's *A Past Revisited*, Guerrero's *Philippine Society and Revolution*, Hurley's *Jungle Patrol*, Ileto's *Pasyon and Revolution*, Malay's "The Sakay Republic," Santos' *Ang Tatlong Napabantog na "Tulisan" sa Pilipinas*, Scott's *Union Obrera Democratica*, Taylor's *The Philippine Insurrection against the United States* (vol. 2), and Watson's "The Christmas Eve Fiasco and a Brief Outline of the

Ricarte and Other Similar Movements"; and the *Reports of the U.S. Philippine Commission* for the years 1904, 1905, 1906, and 1907.

For Macario Sakay, the same materials for Montalan were used, in addition to Abad's "Not Outlaws, but Patriots," Abesamis' "Last Stand," Agoncillo's *Malolos,* Alejandrino's memoirs and his grandson's historical novel (*Insurrectos!*), Almario's "Rebeldeng Barbero," Alzona's *Julio Nakpil and the Philippine Revolution,* Avellana's "Conversations" (on *Sakay,* the film), Corpuz's "The Mischief of the Fourth of July of 1902," Foreman's *The Philippine Islands,* Francisco's "The First Vietnam," Gleeck's recent works (on Laguna in American times, the American Governors-General, and the American half-century in the Philippines), Guerrero-Nakpil's "Sakay," Joaquin's "When Stopped the Revolution?", Mojica's "The Surrender of Macario Sakay," Salamanca's *The Filipino Reaction to American Rule,* Teodoro's "The Tragedy of General Macario Sakay," Villaroel's *Eminent Filipinos,* Yambot's "Sino si Macario Sakay?", and Zaide's *Great Filipinos in History.*

I was not able to read Zaide's 1930 article on Sakay, and I have not seen Avellana's 1939 film either, but I felt licensed to include them—for record purposes and for the sake of future researchers on "bandit" history—together with the supplementary reading materials I have collected and entered in the general bibliography.

ANNOTATED BIBLIOGRAPHY

Abad, Antonio K. *General Macario L. Sakay: Was He a Bandit or a Patriot?* Manila: J.B. Feliciano & Sons, 1955. With an introduction by Teodoro A. Agoncillo.

_____. "Not Outlaws, but Patriots," *Sunday Times Magazine,* 2 March 1947.

Abella, Domingo. *The Flag of Our Fathers.* Manila: Milagros Romualdez Abella, 1977.

Abesamis, Ma. Elena H. "Last Stand," *Sunday Times Magazine,* 22 June 1969.

Achutequi, Pedro S. de, and Miguel A. Bernad. *Aguinaldo and the Revolution of 1896: A Documentary History.* Manila: Ateneo de Manila, 1972.

_____. *Religious Revolution in the Philippines: The Life and Church of Gregorio Aglipay.* Manila: Ateneo de Manila, 1960. Vol. 1.

Agoncillo, Teodoro A. *A Short History of the Philippines.* New York and Toronto: New American Library, 1975.

_____. *The Writings and Trial of Andres Bonifacio.* Manila: Bonifacio Centennial Commission, 1963.

_____. *Malolos: The Crisis of the Republic.* Quezon City: The U.P. Press, 1960.

_____. *The Revolt of the Masses: The Story of Bonifacio and the Katipunan.* Quezon City: The U.P. Press, 1956.

Aguinaldo, Emilio. *Mga Gunita ng Himagsikan.* Manila: Cristina Aguinaldo Suntay, 1964.

_____. *Reseña Veridica de la Revolucion Filipina.* Tarlac: Imprenta del Zacarias Fajardo, 1899. For English translations, see *The Philippine Social Science Review* (May 1941), pp. 179-223; *Historical Bulletin* (January-December 1969), pp. 278-313; and Taylor's *Philippine Insurrection,* Vol. 1, pp. 443-448 and Vol. 3, pp. 4-27.

Alejandrino [y Baluyot], Jose. *Insurrectos!* Manila: Alemar's, 1982. A historical novel on the Philippine Revolution.

Alejandrino [y Magdangal], Jose. *The Price of Freedom.* Manila: M. Colcol Company, 1949. Translated from the original Spanish, *La Senda del Sacrificio,* by Jose M. Alejandrino.

Allen, James S. *The Radical Left on the Eve of War: A Political Memoir.* Quezon City: Foundation for Nationalist Studies, 1985.

Almario, Virgilio S. "Rebeldeng Barbero," *Diyaryo Filipino,* 13 September 1991.

Alvarez, Santiago V. *Ang Katipunan at ang Paghihimagsik.* Manila, 1927(?). Typescript copy in the National Library.

Alzona, Encarnacion. *Galicano Apacible: Profile of a Filipino Patriot.* Published by the heirs of Galicano Apacible, 1971.

_____. *Julio Nakpil and the Philippine Revolution.* Manila: Carmelo & Bauermann, 1964.
    Includes the autobiography of Gregoria de Jesus.

Ancheta, Celedonio A. "Simeon A. Ola (1865-1952)," *Historical Bulletin,* Vol. XII, Nox. 1-4 (January-December 1968).

Archer, Jules. *The Philippines' Fight for Freedom.* London: Crowell-Collier Press, 1970.

Arens, Richard. "The Early Pulahan Movement in Samar," *Leyte-Samar Studies,* Vol. XI, No. 2 (1977).

Aspillera, Paraluman S. (ed.). *Talambuhay ni Lope K. Santos.* Manila: Capitol Publishing House, 1972.

Ataviado, Elias. *The Philippine Revolution in the Bicol Region.* Manila: Encal Press, 1953. Translated from the original Spanish, *Lucha y Libertad,* by Juan T. Ataviado.

Avellana, Lamberto V. "Conversations [on the making of his film *Sakay* in 1939] from Inverness [Studio], Sta. Ana, to Baras, Rizal, in Five Unmelodic Movements," *Sunday Globe Magazine,* 11 June 1989.

_____. *Sakay.* Manila: Filippine Films, 1939. A historical film on the "bandit" and his times.

Baclagon, Uldarico S. *Philippine Campaigns.* Manila: Graphic House, 1952.

Bain, David Haward. *Sitting in Darkness: Americans in the Philippines.* Boston: Houghton Mifflin Company, 1984.

Balein, Jose C. "Encounter in Balangiga," *Weekend Magazine,* 24 August and 31 August 1980.

Barranco, Vicente F. "He Fought with Sakay," *Sunday Times Magazine,* 31 March 1946.

Barrows, David P. *History of the Philippines.* New York: World Book Company, 1924. Revised ed.

Benitez, Conrado. *History of the Philippines.* New York: Ginn and Company, 1954. Revised ed.

Blount, James H. *The American Occupation of the Philippines, 1898-1912.* New York: G.P. Putnam's Sons, 1912. Manila: Malaya Books, 1968.

Borrinaga, Rolando O. "The Pulahan of Leyte: Juan Tamayo," *Philippine Currents,* February 1990.

134

Brillantes, Gregorio C. "That War with the Americans," *Philippines Free Press*, 12 June 1965.

Breihan, Carl W. *Quantrill and His Civil War Guerrillas*. New York: Promontory Press, 1959.

Bresnahan, Roger J. *In Time of Hesitation: American Anti-Imperialists and the Philippine-American War*. Quezon City: New Day Publishers, 1981.

Cabrera, Rod E. "Macario Sakay: The 'Bandit' Was a Hero," *Weekend Magazine*, 15 March 1981.

Campbell, Arthur. *Guerrillas*. London: Arthur Books, 1967.

Carter, Thomas. *Land of the Morning: A Pictorial History of the American Regime*. Manila: Historical Conservation Society, 1990.

_____. *Then and Now*. Manila: Historical Conservation Society, 1983.

Castillo, Erwin. "The Revolution in Cavite," *Sunday Inquirer Magazine*, 28 May, 4 June and 11 June 1989.

_____. "The Life and Times of a Minor Myth," *Asia-Philippines Leader*, 16 June 1972.

Chaput, Donald. "Leyte Leadership in the Revolution: The Mojica-Lukban Issue," *Leyte-Samar Studies*, Vol. IX, No. 1 (1975).

_____. "Founding of the Leyte Scouts," *Leyte-Samar Studies*, Vol. IX, No. 2 (1975).

_____. "The American Press and General Vicente Lukban, Hero of Samar," *Leyte-Samar Studies*, Vol. VIII, No. 1 (1974).

Concepcion, Epifanio. *Memorias de Un Revolucionario*. Iloilo City: National Press, 1949.

Concepcion, Rod F. "Generala," *Woman's Home Companion*, 28 March, 4, 11, 18 and 25 April 1990. A historical narrative on Laguna's rebel heroine.

Constantino, Letizia R. *Recalling the Philippine-American War*. Quezon City: The Education Forum, 1989.

Constantino, Renato. *The Philippines: A Past Revisited*. Quezon City: Tala Publishing Services, 1975.

_____. "Roots of Subservience," *Graphic*, 12 June 1968.

_____. "Origin of a Myth," *Graphic*, 17 April 1968.

Corpuz, O.D. "The Mischief of the Fourth of July of 1902," *Philippines Newsday*, 4 July 1990.

_____. "The Liberating Army of Filipinas," *Philippines Newsday*, 9 October 1989.

Cortes, Rosario Mendoza. *Pangasinan 1901-1986: A Political, Socioeconomic and Cultural History*. Quezon City: New Day Publishers, 1990.

_____. *Pangasinan 1801-1900: The Beginnings of Modernization*. Quezon City: New Day Publishers, 1990.

Cristobal Cruz, Andres. "Sarung Banggi—Awit ng Paglaya?", *Liwayway*, 29 March 1976.

135

Cruz, E. Aguilar. "Orphans of the Katipunan," *Philippines Newsday*, 26, 28, and 30 December 1990.

_____ (tr.). *The War in the Philippines: As Reported by Two French Journalists in 1899.* Manila: National Historical Institute, 1986.

Cruz, Ric de la. "Of the .45 Caliber Pistol and Other Legends," *Who Magazine*, 10 June 1978.

Cullamar, Evelyn Tan. *Babaylanism in Negros: 1896-1907.* Quezon City: New Day Publishers, 1986.

Daroy, Petronilo Bn. "Imperialist Gore," *Graphic*, 23 August 1972.

_____. "Cry, Slaughter!", *Graphic*, 14 June 1972.

Dery, Luis Camara. "From Insurrecto to Bandido," in his *From Ibalon to Sorsogon.* Quezon City: New Day Publishers, 1991.

Devins, John Bancroft. *An Observer in the Philippines.* Boston, New York and Chicago: American Tract Society, 1905.

Dizon, Romeo G. "Huklore," *Philippine Currents*, March 1990.

Elesterio, Fernando G. *Three Essays on Philippine Religious Culture.* Manila: De La Salle University Press, 1989.

Elliot, Charles B. *The Philippines to the End of the Military Regime.* Indianapolis: Bobbs-Merrill Company, 1916.

Fast, Jonathan, and Jim Richardson. *Roots of Dependency: Economic Revolution in 19th Century Philippines.* Quezon City: Foundation for Nationalist Studies, 1979.

Faust, Karl Irving. *Campaigning in the Philippines.* San Francisco: The Hicks-Judd Company, 1899.

Fernandez, Leandro. *The Philippine Republic.* New York: Columbia University Press, 1926.

Foreman, John. *The Philippine Islands.* Hongkong, Shanghai and Singapore: Kelly and Walsh, 1906. 3rd ed.

Foronda, Marcelino A. *Some Notes on Philippine Historiography.* Manila: United Publishing Company, 1972.

Francisco, Luzviminda. "The First Vietnam: The U.S.-Philippine War of 1899," *Bulletin of Concerned Asian Scholars*, Vol. 5, No. 4 (December 1973).

Funtecha, Henry Florida. *American Military Occupation of the Lake Lanao Region, 1901-1913.* Marawi City: Mindanao State University, 1979.

Gagelonia, Pedro A. *The Filipino Historian: Controversial Issues in Philippine History.* Manila: Far Eastern University, 1970.

Galang, Zoilo. *Encyclopedia of the Philippines.* Manila: McCullough Printing Co., 1950. 3rd ed. 10 vols.

Garcia, Mauro (ed.). *Aguinaldo in Retrospect.* Manila: Philippine Historical Association, 1969. With documents on the Philippine-American War.

Garcia, Pantaleon. *Maikling Ulat ng Himagsikan sa Pilipinas.* Manila: Jose Paez Santos, 1930.

Geismar, Maxwell. "Mark Twain on U.S. Imperialism, Racism and Other Enduring Characteristics of the Republic," *Ramparts,* May 1968.

Gianakos, Perry E. *George Ade's Stories of "Benevolent Assimilation."* Quezon City: New Day Publishers, 1985.

Ginsburg, Robert N. "Damn the Insurrectos!", *The Military Review,* January 1964.

Giron, Eric S. "The Trying First Decade of the PC," *Philippine Panorama,* 7 August 1977.

Givens, J.D. *Scenes Taken in the Philippines.* n.p., 1912, unpaged. Pictorial collection.

Gleeck, Lewis E. *The American Governors-General and High Commissioners in the Philippines.* Quezon City: New Day Publishers, 1988.

_____. *The American Half-Century: 1898-1946.* Manila: Historical Conservation Society, 1984.

_____. *Laguna in American Times: Coconuts and Revolucionarios.* Manila: Historical Conservation Society, 1981.

Guerrero, Amado. *Philippine Society and Revolution.* Manila: Pulang Tala Publications, 1971.

Guerrero-Nakpil, Carmen. "Sakay: A Victim of Jaundiced History," *Philippine Daily Express,* 19 September 1976.

Guerrero, Milagros. "Provincial Elites during the Philippine Revolution," in *Philippine Social History* (Quezon City: Ateneo de Manila University, 1982), edited by Alfred McCoy and Edilberto de Jesus.

Historical Calendar. Manila: National Historical Commission, 1970.

Holli, Melvin G. "A View of the American Campaign against 'Filipino Insurgents': 1900," *Philippine Studies,* Vol. XVII, No. 1 (1969).

Hurley, Vic. *Jungle Patrol: The Story of the Philippine Constabulary.* New York: E.P. Dutton and Co., 1938.

Ileto, Reynaldo C. *Critical Questions on Nationalism: A Historian's View.* Manila: De La Salle University, 1986.

_____. "Orators and the Crowd: Philippine Independence Politics, 1910-1914," in *Reappraising an Empire* (Cambridge: Harvard University Press, 1984), edited by Peter Stanley.

_____. "Toward a Local History of the Philippine-American War: The Case of Tiaong, Tayabas (Quezon) Province, 1901-1902." *The Journal of History,* Vol. XXVII, Nos. 1-2 (January-December 1982).

_____. *Pasyon and Revolution: Popular Movements in the Philippines, 1840-1910.* Quezon City: Ateneo de Manila University, 1979.

Joaquin, Nick. *The Aquinos of Tarlac.* Manila: Cacho Hermanos, 1983.
    See especially "Part One: The General" for an account on General Servillano Aquino and the Revolution in Tarlac and Central Luzon.

_____. *Culture and History.* Manila: Solar Publishing Corporation, 1988.
    See especially "Apocalypse and the Revolution" and "The American Interlude."

_____. *A Question of Heroes.* Makati: Ayala Museum, 1977.
      See especially "When Stopped the Revolution?" for an account on General Artemio Ricarte and the "bandit" period of the Philippine-American War.

_____ (tr.). *A Spaniard in Aguinaldo's Army.* Manila: Solar Publishing Corporation, 1986.
      Translated from the military journal of Telesforo Carrasco y Perez.

Jocano, F. Landa. "Ideology and Radical Movements in the Philippines: An Anthropological Overview." *Solidarity,* No. 102 (1985).

Jose, F. Sionil. *Mass.* Manila: Solidaridad Publishing House, 1983.
      A novel on the continuing Philippine Revolution; chronologically, last of the author's Rosales saga.

_____. *Poon.* Manila: Solidaridad Publishing House, 1983.
      A novel on the Philippine Revolution; chronologically, first of the author's Rosales saga.

_____ (ed.). "The Huks in Retrospect: A Failed Bid for Power." *Solidarity,* No. 102 (1985).
      Record of a seminar participated in by Casto Alejandrino, Jesus Lava, Alfredo B. Saulo, and Luis Taruc.

Jose, Vivencio R. *The Rise and Fall of Antonio Luna.* Manila: Solar Publishing Corporation, 1991. Filipiniana Reprint Series.

_____. "Workers' Response to American Rule: Manila 1900- 1935." *The Journal of History,* Vol. XXVII, Nos. 1-2 (January- December 1982).

Kalaw, Maximo M. *The Filipino Rebel.* Manila: Filipiniana Book Guild, 1964. Reprint.
      A historical novel on the Philippine Revolution.

Kalaw, Teodoro M. *The Philippine Revolution.* Manila: Manila Book Company, 1925. Mandaluyong (Rizal): Jorge B. Vargas Filipiniana Foundation, 1969. Reprint.

Karnow, Stanley. *In Our Image: America's Empire in the Philippines.* New York: Random House, 1989. Reprinted in the Philippines by National Book Store.

Kasandugo (pseud.). *Ang Katipunan at si Gat Andres Bonifacio.*
      Typescript, n.d., in the National Library.

Kelly, Amzi B. *The Killing of General Noriel.* Manila: National Conservation Society, 1987. Reprint of the original 1916 title, *General Mariano Noriel, Innocent.*

Lachica, Eduardo. *Huk: Philippine Agrarian Society in Revolt.* Manila: Solidaridad Publishing House, 1971.

Lapeña-Bonifacio, Amelia. *"Seditious" Tagalog Playwrights: Early American Occupation.* Manila: Zarzuela Foundation of the Philippines, 1972.

Larkin, John A. *The Pampangans: Colonial Society in a Philippine Province.* Berkeley: University of California Press, 1972.

Laus, Emiliano L. *The Ten Most Outstanding Filipino National Leaders.* Manila: National Printing Co., 1951.

Legarda, Benito J. "The First Shot That Triggered the Fil-American War in February 1899 Was Fired in Balic-Balic, Not San Juan (A Neighborhood Chronicle)," *Mr. & Ms. Magazine*, 2 and 9 February 1988.

Leroy, James A. *The Americans in the Philippines*. Boston and New York: Houghton Mifflin Co., 1914. 2 vols.

Leveriza, Jose P. *Rage in the Hearts*. Quezon City: New Day Publishers, 1988.
   A historical novel on the Ola campaign of the Philippine- American War in Bicol.

Lumbera, Bienvenido. "Aguilar, Abad at Gatmaitan: Tatlong Manunulat sa Pakikibaka (1900-1912)." *The Philippine Collegian Folio*, First Semester (1970-1971).

Luzviminda (pseud.). "Pahalaw na Salaysay sa Kabuhayan ni Agueda Esteban at de la Cruz," *Bulletin of the Philippine Historical Association*, No. 1 (July 1957).

Mabini, Apolinario. *Letters*. Manila: National Heroes Commission, 1965. With a preface by Carlos Quirino and annotations by Teodoro M. Kalaw.

_____. *The Philippine Revolution*. Manila: Loyal Press, 1935.

McClennan, Marshall S. *The Central Luzon Plain: Land and Society on the Inland Frontier*. Quezon City: Alemar's-Phoenix Publishing House, 1980.

Majul, Cesar Adib. "La Liga Filipina: Rizal, Bonifacio and Mabini," *Bulletin of the Philippine Historical Association*, No. 5 (September 1958).

Malay, Armando J. "The Sakay Republic." *Weekly Women's Magazine*, 15 March 1957.

Manuel, E. Arsenio. *Dictionary of Philippine Biography*. Manila: Filipiniana Publications, 1955 (Vol. 1) and 1970 (Vol. 2).

Mao Tse-Tung, and Che Guevarra. *Guerilla Warfare*. London: Cassell and Company, 1962. With a foreword by Basil H. Liddell Hart.

May, Glenn Anthony. *A Past Recovered*. Quezon City: New Day Publishers, 1987.
   See especially "Part Three: Rethinking the Philippine- American War" for a full account of the Malvar campaign in Batangas.

_____. *Social Engineering in the Philippines*. Quezon City: New Day Publishers, 1984. Reprint.

Medina, B. S. *The Primal Passion*. Manila: Centro Escolar University, 1976.

Milan, Primitivo C. "General Simeon Ola." *Philippines Free Press*, 28 May 1955.

Miller, Stuart Creighton. *"Benevolent Assimilation": The American Conquest of the Philippines, 1899-1903*. New Haven and London: Yale University Press, 1982.

Minutes of the Katipunan. Manila: National Historical Institute, 1978.

Misa, Arturo Ma. "Emilio Jacinto as Meat Merchant," *Sunday Times Magazine*, 4 June 1972.

Mojica, Abelardo P. "The Surrender of Macario Sakay," *This Week Magazine*, 7 May 1950.

Molina, Antonio M. *The Philippines Through the Centuries.* Manila: University of Santo Tomas Press, 1960. 2 vols.

Ocampo, Ambeth R. *Looking Back.* Pasig (Metro Manila): Anvil Publishing, Inc., 1990.

_____. "Mark Twain on the Fil-American War," *Weekend Magazine,* 28 September 1986.

_____. "America's Forgotten War," *Weekend Magazine,* 29 June 1986.

Ocampo, Nilo S. "Kawing sa Rebolusyon: Tayabas, 1896-1898," *Diliman Review,* Vol. 36, No. 4 (1988).

Ochosa, Orlino A. *The Tinio Brigade: Anti-American Resistance in the Ilocos Provinces 1899-1901.* Quezon City: New Day Publishers, 1989.

_____. "Emilio Jacinto *Pingkian:* Putting the Jigsaw Pieces on the Biographical Puzzle of the Model Katipunero," *Diliman Review,* Vol. 37, No. 3 (1989).

_____. "Cavite's Peasant Hero: Shattering the Myth of Julian Montalan as Bandit and Scamp," *Diliman Review,* Vol. 37, No. 2 (1989).

    Reprinted with permission as Chapter 2 of this present work, with an additional section on Gregorio Porto's story of Montalan's "treasures."

_____. "Big Black Brother: Remembering David Fagan, a Black Guerrilla in the Philippine-American War," *Diliman Review,* Vol. 36, No. 4 (1988).

_____. "Himagsikan ng mga Tulisan," *Diliman Review,* Vol. 36, No. 3 (1988).

_____. "Gen. Luciano San Miguel: A Rebel to the End," *Mirror Magazine,* 13 November 1965.

Onorato, Michael P. "The United States and the Philippine Independence Movement," *Solidarity,* Vol. V, No. 9 (1970).

Paredes, Ruby R. (ed.). *Philippine Colonial Democracy.* Quezon City: Ateneo de Manila University Press, 1989.

    See especially "The Origins of National Politics: Taft and the Partido Federal."

Pastrana, Apolinar. *A Friar's Account of the Philippine Revolution in Bicol.* Quezon City: Franciscan Friary of St. Gregory the Great, 1980.

Pecson, Geronima, and Maria Racelis. *Tales of the American Teachers in the Philippines.* Manila: Carmelo & Bauermann, 1959.

Philippine Historical Papers, 1952-1953.

    Bound manuscript compilation of local histories of all towns in the Philippines, kept in the National Library. See especially volumes for Cavite, Batangas, Laguna, Rizal, and Bulacan.

Philippine Insurgent Records. Original documents captured from "insurrectos" during the Philippine-American War.

    Now kept in the National Library Filipiniana Division filed as "Philippine Revolutionary Papers. See especially papers of the Katipunan and "Selected Documents."

Pilar y Castaneda, Pio del. *Biografia.* Manuscript. Manila, 1929.

    The Ronquillo Collection copy in the National Library is incomplete.

Pomeroy, William. *American Neo-Colonialism: Its Emergence in the Philippines and Asia.* New York: International Publishers, 1970. Manila: Cacho Hermanos, 1985. Filipiniana Reprint Series.

Porto, Gregorio [as told to Vivencio Porto]. "Buried Treasures Lie Untouched in Cavite," *Manila Times Daily Magazine,* 2 January 1960.

Quezon, Manuel Luis. *The Good Fight.* New York and London: D. Appleton-Century Co., 1946.

Quintos, Felipe. *Breves Relatos de la Revolucion de las Filipinas.* Alaminos (Pangasinan), 1947.
Typescript copy in the National Library.

Quirino, Carlos. *Quezon: Paladin of Philippine Freedom.* Manila: Filipiniana Book Guild, 1971.

_____. *The Young Aguinaldo.* Manila: Regal Printing Co., 1969.

Quirino, Jose A. "The Three Faces of the Hero: A Legend of the Vibora," *Philippines Free Press,* 8 June 1968.

Quisumbing, Jose R. *The American Occupation of Cebu: Warwick Barracks, 1899-1917.* Quezon City: Progressive Printing Palace, 1983.

Ramos-De Leon, Lilia. "The Filipino Geronimo, a Super General, was the Nemesis of Gen. Lawton," *Philippine Panorama,* 7 July 1981.

Regalado, Felix B., and Quintin B. Franco. *History of Panay.* Iloilo City: Central Philippine University, 1973.

Reports of the U.S. Philippine Commission. Washington, D.C.: Government Printing Office. Volumes for the years 1903, 1904, 1905, 1906, and 1907.

Reyes, Isabelo de los. *La Religion del Katipunan.* Madrid: Imprenta lit. del J. Corrales, 1900. 2nd ed.

Reyes, Pedrito. *Pictorial History of the Philippines.* Quezon City: Capitol Publishing House, 1952.

Ricarte, Artemio. *Memoirs.* Manila: National Heroes Commission, 1963. With an Introduction by Armando J. Malay.

_____. *The Hispano-Philippine Revolution.* Yokohama: (published by the author), 1926.

Robinson, Albert G. *The Philippines: The War and the People.* New York: McClure, Phillips and Company, 1901.

Robles, Eliodoro G. *The Philippines in the Nineteenth Century.* Quezon City: Malaya Books, Inc., 1969. With an Introduction by Teodoro A. Agoncillo.

Romero, Ma. Fe Hernaez. *Negros Occidental between Two Foreign Powers, 1898-1909.* Bacolod City: Negros Occidental Historical Commission, 1974.

Rosca, Ninotchka. "Rayadillo and Toledo Steel," *Asia-Philippines Leader,* 12 June 1971.

Roth, Russell. *Muddy Glory: America's "Indian Wars" in the Philippines 1899-1935.* West Hanover, Massachusetts: Christopher Publishing House, 1981.

Salamanca, Bonifacio S. *The Filipino Reaction to American Rule, 1901-1913.* Quezon City: New Day Publishers, 1984. Reprint.

Salanga, Alfrredo Navarro. *The Aglipay Question: Literary and Historical Studies of the Life and Times of Gregorio Aglipay.* Quezon City: Crisis Foundation, Inc., 1982.

Santos, Epifanio de los. *The Revolutionists: Aguinaldo, Bonifacio, Jacinto.* Manila: National Historical Commission, 1973. With annotations and an Introduction by Teodoro A. Agoncillo.

Santos, Jose P. *Buhay at mga Sinulat ni Emilio Jacinto.* Manila: Jose Paez Santos, 1935.

_____. *Ang Tatlong Napabantog na "Tulisan" sa Pilipinas.* Gerona (Tarlac): Jose Paez Santos, 1936.

Saulo, Alfredo B. *The Truth about Aguinaldo and Other Heroes.* Quezon City: Phoenix Publishing House, 1987.

Schirmer, Daniel B. *Republic or Empire: American Resistance to the Philippine War.* Cambridge, Massachusetts: Schenkman Publishing Co., 1972.

_____, and Stephen Rosskam Shalom. *The Philippines Reader.* Quezon City: Ken, Inc., 1987. Reprint.
        A history of colonialism, neocolonialism, dictatorship, and resistance.

Schott, Joseph L. *The Ordeal of Samar.* Manila: Solar Publishing Corporation, 1987. Filipiniana Reprint Series.

Schreurs, Peter. *Angry Days in Mindanao: The Philippine Revolution and the War against the U.S. in Northeast and East Mindanao, 1897-1901.* Cebu City: San Carlos Publications, 1987.

Schumacher, John. *The Propaganda Movement, 1880-1895.* Manila: Solidaridad Publishing House, 1973.

_____. *Revolutionary Clergy.* Quezon City: Ateneo de Manila University Press, 1981.

Scott, William Henry. "Guerrilla Padre," *National Midweek,* 1 and 8 June 1988.

_____. *Ilocano Responses to American Aggression, 1900-1901.* Quezon City: New Day Publishers, 1986.

_____. "A Minority Reaction to American Imperialism: Isabelo de los Reyes," *The Journal of History,* Vol. XXVII, Nos. 1-2 (January-December 1982).

_____. "The Union Obrera Democratica, First Filipino Labor Union," *Philippine Social Sciences and Humanities Review,* Vol. XLVII, Nos. 1-4 (January-December 1983).

Serrano, Leopoldo R. "A Brief History of Caloocan," *Bulletin of the Philippine Historical Association,* No. 3 (March 1958).

_____. "News from Up Front as Seen by the Republic's Reporters," *Sunday Times Magazine,* 2 January 1962.

Sexton, William T. *Soldiers in the Sun.* Harrisburg, Pennsylvania: The Military Service Publishing Co., 1939.

Sison, Jose Ma. "My Ancestors in the Revolution: The Sisons and the Serranos in the Struggle against Colonialism and Imperialism." *National Midweek*, 2 July 1986.

Sonza, Demy P. "The Mysterious Death of General Pascual Magbanua," *Philippines Free Press*, 19 November 1961.

_____. *Visayan Fighters for Freedom*. Iloilo City: Yuhum Press, 1962.

Steinberg, David Joel. "An Ambiguous Legacy: Years at War in the Philippines," *Pacific Affairs*, Vol. XLV, No. 2 (1972).

St. Clair, Francis. *The Katipunan, or the Rise and Fall of the Filipino Commune*. Manila: Tip. "Amigo del Pais," 1902.

Storey, Moorefield, and Marcial P. Lichauco. *The Conquest of the Philippines by the United States, 1898-1925*. New York: G.P. Putnam's Sons, 1926.

Sturtevant, David. "Guardia de Honor: Revitalization within the Revolution," *Asian Studies*, Vol. IV, No. 2 (1966).

_____. "Rural Discord: The Peasantry and Nationalism," *Solidarity*, Vol. VII, No. 2, 1972)

Taber, Robert. *The War of the Flea: A Study of Guerrilla Warfare Theory and Practice*. London: Paladin, 1977.

Tan, Antonio S. "The Ideology of Pedro Abad Santos' Socialist Party," *Solidarity*, No. 102 (1985).

Tan, Samuel K. *The Filipino Muslim Armed Struggle, 1900-1972*. Manila: Filipinas Foundation, 1977.

Taylor, John R.M. *The Philippine Insurrection against the United States*. Pasay City: Eugenio Lopez Foundation, 1971-1973. 5 vols.
    See especially Vols. 1, 2 and 5.

Teodoro, Luis V. "The Tragedy of General Macario Sakay," in *Filipino Heritage*. Manila: Lahing Filipino Publishing, 1978: Vol. 9.

Trafton, William Oliver. *We Thought We Could Whip Them in Two Weeks*. Quezon City: New Day Publishers, 1990. Edited with notes by William Henry Scott.

Ty-Casper, Linda. *Ten Thousand Seeds*. Quezon City: Ateneo de Manila University Press, 1987.
    A historical novel on the Philippine-American War.

Veneracion, Jaime B. *Merit or Patronage: A History of the Philippine Civil Service*. Quezon City: Great Books Trading, 1988.

Villa, Simeon and Santiago Barcelona. *Aguinaldo's Odyssey: As Told in the Diaries of Col. Simeon Villa and Dr. Santiago Barcelona*. Manila: Bureau of Public Libraries, 1963. With an introduction by Carlos Quirino.

Villanueva, Alejo L. *Bonifacio's Unfinished Revolution*. Quezon City: New Day Publishers, 1989.

Villanueva, Honesto A. "The Case of Apolinario Mabini in Guam," *Bulletin of the Philippine Historical Association*, No. 3 (March 1958).

Villaroel, Hector, *et al. Eminent Filipinos.* Manila: National Historical Commission, 1965. With a preface by Carlos Quirino.

Watson, William Brecknock. "The Christmas Eve Fiasco and a Brief Outline of the Ricarte and Other Similar Movements," In *Memoirs of Artemio Ricarte.*

Welch, Richard E. *Response to Imperialism: The United States and the Philippine-American War, 1899-1902.* Chapel Hill: University of North Carolina, 1987. 2nd printing.

Wilcox, Marrion (ed.). *Harper's History of the War in the Philippines.* New York: Harper and Brothers, 1900.

Willis, Henry Parker. *Our Philippine Problem: A Study of American Colonial Policy.* New York: Henry Holt and Co., 1905.

Wolff, Leon. *Little Brown Brother.* New York: Doubleday, 1961. Manila: Erehwon Press, 1971.

Yambot, Efren. "Sino si Macario Sakay?", *Graphic,* 16 February 1972.

Yap-Diangco, Robert T. *The Filipino Guerrilla Tradition.* Manila: MCS Enterprises, 1971.

Young, Kenneth Ray. "Atrocities and War Crimes: The Cases of Major Waller and General Smith," *Leyte-Samar Studies,* Vol. XII, No. 1 (1978).

_____. "Guerrilla Warfare: Balangiga Revisited," *Leyte-Samar Studies,* Vol. XI, No. 1 (1977).

Zaide, Gregorio F. *Manila during the Revolutionary Period.* Manila: National Historical Commission, 1973.

_____. *Great Filipinos in History.* Manila: Verde Book Store, 1970.

_____. *Philippine Political and Cultural History.* Manila: Philippine Education Company, 1957. Revised ed. 2 vols.

_____. *The Philippine Revolution.* Manila: Modern Book Company, 1954.

_____. *History of the Katipunan.* Manila: Loyal Press, 1939.

_____. "Macario L. Sakay, President of the Last Tagalog Republic," *Sunday Tribune Magazine,* 2 March 1930.

POSTSCRIPT

AS *"BANDOLEROS"* went to press, Ateneo de Manila University published Paula Malay's long-awaited English translation of the Alvarez memoirs, New Day came out with a reprint of Glenn May's fine book on the war in Batangas, Anvil printed Erwin Castillo's metafiction on the Cavite "patriot bandidos," U.P. Press produced Isagani Medina's pre-1896 history tribute to his native Cavite (highlighted by his masterpiece on "Tulisanismo"), Raymond Red made an acclaimed new film biography of Sakay based on "new historiography," and I discovered—better late than never—a few other good materials that I missed out, which otherwise would have been helpful to me. And which is the reason for this bibliographical postscript:

Aguinaldo Shrine. *96th Anniversary of the Proclamation of Philippine Independence, June 12, 1994.* Souvenir Brochure.
    Contains thumbnail biographical sketches of Cavite's revolutionary heroes. The portion on Luciano San Miguel, attributing its source to an unpublished manuscript by Sol H. Gwekoh entitled "General Luciano San Miguel" [1973] in the U.P. Main Library Archives Section, gives vital data on the date (January 7, 1875) and place (Noveleta, Cavite) of San Miguel's birth. From this detail we learn that San Miguel belongs to the Revolution's impressive roll of "boy generals"—in the same league of Manuel Tinio, Leandro Fullon, Emilio Jacinto, Gregorio del Pilar, Mamerto and Benito Natividad, Flaviano Yengko, Mariano Riego de Dios, Pascual Magbanua, Servillano Aquino, and others.

Almario, Virgilio S. *Panitikan ng Rebolusyon(g 1896): Isang Paglingon at Katipunan ng mga Akda nina Bonifacio at Jacinto.* Manila: Sentrong Pangkultura ng Pilipinas, 1993.

Alvarez, Santiago V. *The Katipunan and the Revolution: Memoirs of a General.* Quezon City: Ateneo de Manila University Press, 1992.
    Translated from the original Tagalog, *Ang Katipunan at ang Paghihimag-*

sik [1927], by Paula Carolina Malay.

Castillo, Erwin. *The Firewalkers*. Pasig (Metro Manila): Anvil Publishing, Inc., 1992.
>Nick Joaquin describes the book: "An epic of Cavite Heroico, in the days of the Gringo, the Scout, the patriot 'bandidos'—and civilize 'em with a Krag!"

Constantino, Renato. *History: Myths and Reality*. Quezon City: Karrel, Inc. [1991?].

Corpuz, O. D. *The Roots of the Filipino Nation*. Quezon City: Aklahi Foundation, Inc., 1989. 2 vols.

De Guzman, Domingo Castro. "Theorizing the Theories of the Anti-Colonial Revolution," *Diliman Review*, Vol. 39, No. 3 (1991).

Del Mundo, Clodualdo, Jr. *Tatlong Dulang Pampelikula*. Manila: De la Salle University Press, 1992.
>The third *dula* in the book, "Alyas Raha Matanda," co-authored with brother Herky del Mundo, presents an authentic movie screenplay of the Sakay story.

Filipinos in History. Manila: National Historical Institute, 1989-1992. 3 vols.
>This is an expanded, improved version of *Eminent Filipinos*, published by the National Historical Commission in 1965.

Foronda, Marcelino A., Jr. *Kasaysayan: Studies on Local and Oral History*. Manila: De La Salle University Press, 1991.

Gealogo, Francis A. "Ang mga Taong Labas, ang Kabayanihan, at ang Diskurso ng Kapangyarihan at Kasaysayan," *Diliman Review*, Vol. 38, No. 1 (1990).
>This special history issue of *DR*, edited by Jaime Veneracion, also includes fresh views on the Filipino-American War in Bulacan, Leyte, and Tayabas.

Guillermo, Alice G. "Interpretations on the Revolution of 1896," *Diliman Review*, Vol. 40, No. 1 (1992).

Kerkvliet, Melinda Tria. *Manila Workers Unions, 1900-1950*. Quezon City: New Day Publishers, 1992.

Laurie, Clayton D. "The Philippine Scouts: America's Colonial Army, 1899-1913," *Philippine Studies*, No. 37 (Second Quarter, 1989).

Lim, Jaime An. *Literature and Politics: The Colonial Experience in Nine Philippine Novels*. Quezon City: New Day Publishers, 1993. With a foreword by Leonard Casper.

Llanes, Ferdinand (ed.). *Katipunan: Isang Pambansang Kilusan*. Quezon City: Trinitas Publishing, Inc., 1994.

_____. *Pagbabalik sa Bayan: Mga Lektura sa Kasaysayan ng Historiyograpiya at Pagkabansang Pilipino*. Manila: Rex Book Store, 1993.

Mangahas, Fe B. "Ang Kababaihan sa Kasaysayang Pilipino," *Diliman Review*, Vol. 39, No. 3 (1991).

Marasigan, Vicente. *A Banahaw Guru: Symbolic Deeds of Agapito Illustrisimo*. Quezon City: Ateneo de Manila University Press, 1985.

Matatag (pseud.). *History of One of the Initiators of the Philippine Revolution.* Manila: National Historical Institute, 1988. Translated with notes from the original Spanish,*Historia de Uno de los Iniciadores de la Revolucion Filipina* [1899], by O. D. Corpuz.

This is the apologetic "memoirs" of Gen. Antonino Guevarra y Mendoza, obviously written to humor Aguinaldo when he was in power (and while Guevarra was an area commander of a Bicol province), since Matatag's well-known sympathies for the *Supremo* in 1896-97, as well as his collaboration with Jacinto's "katipunization" of Laguna, are too glaringly omitted. Use, therefore, with caution.

May, Glenn Anthony. *Battle for Batangas: A Philippine Province at War.* Quezon City: New Day Publishers, 1993. Reprint.

Medina, Isagani R. *Cavite Before the Revolution (1571-1896).* Quezon City: [U.P.] CSSP Publications, 1994.

See especially the chapter on "Tulisanismo," pp. 59-106.

Ocampo, Ambeth R. *Aquinaldo's Breakfast and More "Looking Back" Essays.* Pasig (Metro Manila): Anvil Publishing, Inc., 1993.

Pomeroy, William J. *The Forest: A Personal Record of the Huk Guerrilla Struggle in the Philippines.* Metro Manila: Solar Books, 1994. Filipiniana Reprint Series.

Red, Raymond. *Sakay,* Manila: Alpha Omega Productions, 1993.

A "new historiography" film version of the hero, based on a screenplay by Ian Victorino.

Riggs, Arthur Stanley. *The Filipino Drama (1905).* Manila: Intramuros Administration, 1981. With an introduction by Doreen G. Fernandez.

Salazar, Zeus A. *Ang Pagsalakay ni Bonifacio sa Maynila.* Quezon City: Miranda Bookstore, 1994.

Santiago, Lilia Quindoza. "Ang Kilusang Feminista at ang Katipunan," *Diliman Review,* Vol. 40, No. 1 (1992).

Santos, Angelito L. *Looking Out for Indio Jones: An Essay on Philippine Nationalism and Culture.* Quezon City: Foundation for Nationalist Studies [1991?].

Schult, Volker. "Revolution and War in Mindoro, 1898-1903," *Philippine Studies,* No. 41 (First Quarter, 1993).

Simbulan, Roland. *The Continuing Struggle for an Independent Philippine Foreign Policy.* Manila: Nuclear Free Philippine Coalition, 1991.

Sullivan, Rodney J. *Exemplar of Americanism: The Philippine Career of Dean C. Worcester.* Quezon City: New Day Publishers, 1992.

Swick, Jim (ed.). *Mark Twain's Weapons of Satire: Anti-Imperialist Writings on the Philippine-American War.* Syracuse, New York: Syracuse University Press, 1992. Reprinted in the Philippines by Popular Book Store.

Totanes, Stephen Henry S. "Sorsogon's Principalia and the Policy of Pacification, 1900-1903," *Philippine Studies,* No. 38 (Fourth Quarter, 1990).

147

INDEX

Abacan River, San Miguel's 1899 defense of, 14

Abad, Antonio K., 52, 63, 76, 77, 100, 107, 133; quoted on Felizardo's poisoning incident, 66; misreads Pio del Pilar's account on Sakay, 81; quoted on Sakay's 1903 manifesto, 77, 96, 100; quotes Leon Villafuerte on Sakay's 1906 "capture," 108-109

Abad Santos, Pedro (Perico), as *Socialista*, 128, 129

Abel and Cain, 21

Abesamis, Maria Elena H., quoted on Sakay, 76, 132

Abueg, Capt. Moises, fights under San Miguel, 12

Aglipay, Padre Gregorio, 20, 29, 67, 127

Aglipayanos, 25, 125, 127

Agoncillo, Teodoro A., ix, x; 127, quoted on San Miguel's 1898 role, 7; on Sakay, 76, 77, 79, 111

Aguinaldistas, 22, 26, 34, 91

Aguinaldo, Gen. Baldomero, 31, 34

Aguinaldo, Gen. Emilio ("Magdalo"), ix, x, 4, 6, 13, 17, 20, 23, 27, 31, 35, 49, 53, 54, 78, 80, 87, 89, 91, 113; as Generalissimo/President of the Republic, 15, 17, 19, 33, 37, 60, 85, 88, 100; quoted on San Miguel's 1898 role, 7; promotes San Miguel to general, 13; his Paruao River Line, 14-15; San Miguel's letter from Alaminos, 19; his 1901 capture, 23, 29; on Montalan's bravery, 52; pleads for Montalan's life, 71; passes fictional "torch" to Sakay, 91; Prescott Jernegan's "bandit" slur, 104; his

picture, 92, 114 photo

Aguinaldos, as Magdalo partisans, 131

Alaminos (Zambales), 17, 18

Alba, Major, and San Miguel in Zambales, 22

Albay, "zona" in, 67, 68

Alejandrino (y Baluyot), Jose, quoted on his novel, 91, 92

Alejandrino (y Magdangal), Gen. Jose, as "good *ilustrado*," xii; with San Miguel in Zambales, 16, 21; commanding general for Pangasinan, 22; recalls Colonel Baker's cruelties, 68; his grandson's *burgis* view of Sakay, 91, 92

Ali Baba, 59

Alfonso (Cavite), Col. Masigla fights P.C. in, 64, 105

Almeida, Lucino, as "good *ilustrado*," xii

Allen, Gen. Henry T., as P.C. chief, 35, 38, 58, 93, 119 photo

Alvarez, Major, killed in 1904 Alfonso encounter, 64

Alvarez, Gen. Mariano, 87

Alvarez, Gen. Pascual, 29, 87

Alvarez, Gen. Santiago ("Apoy"), 5, 6, 37, 85, 88, 107; as *Magdiwang* generalissimo, 29, 87, 126; as *Bonifacista* against civil war, 29, 87; on Bonifacio-Malinis incident, 80; on Miguel Ramos "Bulalakaw," 85; as Partido Nacionalista president, 37, 86, 88, 126; alias "Apoy," 87, 114; on Francisco Carreon in Cavite, 98; as *Makabuhay* leader, 127; his picture, 114 photo

Alvarezes, as *Magdiwang* partisans, 6, 28, 55, 87, 115

149

150

158

160

Tandang Sora, snobbed by the Republic, x

Tanggulan movement, Patricio Dionisio's, 128

Tarlac, 7, 8, 10, 11, 14, 16, 29

Tatlong Napabantog na "Tulisan" sa Pilipinas, Ang, Santos's, 84

Taumbakal, in the 1587 Tondo "katipunan," 82

Taylor, Capt. John R. M., quoted on 1899 Filipino retreat from San Juan, 10, 12; on Aguinaldo-Manalang conflict, 11, 12; on San Miguel Brigade's exploits, 11-13; On San Miguel's Zambales papers, 16, 20; on Licerio Geronimo's 1898 role, 34, misspells Montalan's name, 50; on Sakay's "Dapitan" papers, 55, 83, 84

Taytay (Morong/Rizal), 10, 37

Teatro Zorrilla, 104

Tejeros, 1897 revolutionary assembly at, 5, 29, 52, 55, 88

Teresa (Morong/Rizal), Sakay's 1904 raid on, 102

Terpsichore, 9

Tiagong Akyat, 59

Tiburcio (of Mariveles), in Ricartista plot, 126

Tierra Virgen (Isabela), 29

Tinio, Gen. Manuel, 16; as "true *republicano,*" 20

Tinio Brigade, 126

Tioco, Norman, artist, v

Tirad Pass (Ilocos Sur), 44, 45

Tirona, Gen. Daniel, 20, 23

Tirona brothers, as Magdalo partisans, 135

tirong, Montalan and Oruga as, 99

Tolentino, Aurelio, 84, 88, 93; in 1900 KKK revival, 20; as J*unta de Amigos* leader, 24, 83; in the Partido Nacionalista, 86, 88; as Ricartista, 101 footnote; his death in 1911, 127

Tomines, Col. Manuel, 125, 126; hanged by the Americans, 125

Tondo, x, 28, 29, 32, 37, 51, 52, 54, 55, 77, 78, 79, 80, 82, 88, 89, 95, 97, 98, 99, 101, 113, 126; in 1587 conspiracy, 82; as 1900 underground hub, 82-83 (*see* also *Katagalugan*)

Torres, Pantaleon, in the Partido Nacionalista, 86, 88; in 1906 Quiapo meeting of *nacionalistas,* 126

Trece Martires (Cavite), Montalan's "treasures"(?) in, 61

Trias, Gen. Mariano, 24, 29, 31, 52, 53, 63, 66, 68, 71, 96, 115; as Cavite governor under the Americans, 63, 66; blacklisted by guerrillas, 66; San Francisco de Malabon named after him, 51, 72

Trias, Mrs. (Maria?), Felizardo's kidnap of, 66, 70

Trozo, as KKK council, 78, 83, 84, 97; as urban guerrilla "hotbed," 83

True Version of the Revolution, Aguinaldo's, 7

Tuliahan River (Novaliches), 11

"tulisanes," 18, 96 (*see* "bandoleros" and "ladrones")

Twilley, Lt. H.R., "whipped" by San Miguelistas, 36

Union Obrera Democratica, 25, 131 (*see* also *obreros*)

United States, 35, 45, 50, 57, 105, 106, 127 (*see* also America)

U.S. Army, 57, 61, 63, 68, 92

U.S. Cavalry, 11, 57, 67

U.S. Congress, 106

U.S. Fleet, 31

U.S. imperialism (*see* American imperialism)

U.S. Philippine Commission, 52, 56, 58, 69, 104, 106, 131

Utah Battery, at the 1899 battles in Sta. Mesa, 9, 11

Valenzuela, Pio, as KKK *veterano,* 144 photo

Van Schaick, Col. Louis, in Sakay's 1906 "capture," 70, 108, 110

Vega, Col. Lucio de iv, v, 69, 71, 109, 110, 111; leads 1905 Taal raid, 64, 65, 105; "Unsavory quartet," 77; hanged by the Americans, 75, 111, 122, 126; his picture, 120 photo

"Vibora," xiii, 4, 24, 45, 54, 101, 104, 114, 124 (*see* also Ricarte, Artemio)

Vicente, Rufino, as Ricartista, 127

Victorino, Modesto, as Ricartista, 127

164

OTHER NEW DAY BOOKS
ON THE PHILIPPINE-AMERICAN WAR
AND THE AMERICAN COLONIAL PERIOD

Abaya, Hernando J. *The CLU Story, Fifty Years of Struggle for Civil Liberties*

Bresnahan, Roger J. *In Time of Hesitation: American Anti-Imperialists and the Philippine-American War*

Cortes, Rosario Mendoza. *Pangasinan 1901-1986: A Political, Socio-economic and Cultural History*

Cullamar, Evelyn Tan. *Babaylanism in Negros: 1896-1907*

Fry, Howard T. *A History of the Mountain Province*

Gianakos, Perry E. *George Ade's "Stories of 'Benevolent Assimilation'"*

Gleeck, Lewis E. *The American Governors-General and High Commissioners in the Philippines*

    The American Half-Century (1898-1946)

Gowing, Peter Gordon. *Mandate in Moroland, The American Government of Muslim Filipinos, 1899-1920*

Halsema, E. J. *Colonial Engineer, A Biography*

Jenista, Frank Lawrence. *The White Apos: American Governors on the Cordillera Central*

Kerkvliet, Melinda Tria. *Manila Workers' Unions, 1900-1950*

Kwantes, Anne C. *Presbyterian Missionaries in the Philippines: Conduits of Social Change, 1899-1910*

Leveriza, Jose P. *Rage in the Hearts: A Historical Novel*

May, Glenn Anthony. *Battle for Batangas: A Philippine Province at War*

    A Past Recovered: Essays on Philippine History and Historiography

    Social Engineering in the Philippines, The Aims, Execution, and Impact of American Colonial Policy, 1900-1913

Ochosa, Orlino A. *Pio del Pilar and Other Heroes The Tinio Brigade: Anti-American Resistance in the Ilocos Provinces, 1899-1901*

Salamanca, Bonifacio S. *The Filipino Reaction to American Rule, 1901-1913*

Scott, William Henry. *Ilocano Responses to American Aggression, 1900-1901*

    The Union Obrera Democratica: First Filipino Labor Union

Sevilla, Victor J. *Justices of the Supreme Court of the Philippines, Their Lives and Outstanding Decisions, Volume One: 1901-1942*

Sheridan, Richard Brinsley. *The Filipino Martyrs: A Story of the Crime of February 4, 1899*

Sullivan, Rodney J. *Exemplar of Americanism: The Philippine Career of Dean C. Worcester*

Trafton, William Oliver. *We Thought We Could Whip Them in Two Weeks*